The Yacht America

in Florida's Civil War

Other Titles by Jack Owen
Palm Beach – An Irreverent Guide
Palm Beach – An Intimate Guide
The Jekyll Island Enigma

Other Titles by Jack M D Owen
Midshipman Porter – In Harms Way
Up & Down the Ditch – with
Murphy's Law
David Porter, *Philadelphia*
and The Barbary Pirates

The yacht *America* in peace and war

The Yacht *America*, in Florida's Civil War

Jack M D Owen

Old Book Shop Publication, Palm Beach

ISBN-13: 978-0938673156
ISBN-10: 0938673157

Printed in the United States of America

Acknowledgments

I would like to thank all who helped me compile this yarn.

Normally this is where the names, titles and affiliations of the many folks who have aided in unearthing material would be cited.

However, memories are long and feuds determine - to this day - who will be invited to births, marriages and deaths in Old Florida families.

In the interest of continued peace and survival I have opted to redact any reference which would fan the flames of further conflict.

Thanks to all of you.

YOU know who you are!

Jack M D Owen - writer

Table of CONTENTS

Prelude

Part I: The Challenge
Chapter 1   *America* Sets Forth
Chapter 2   A Challenge to the Best
Chapter 3   The Race

Part II: Florida
Chapter 1   Wilderness
Chapter 2   Schism
Chapter 3   Winston Waylaid

Part III: Midshipman in Navy Blue
Chapter 1   Midshipman in Navy Blue
Chapter 2   Homesick
Chapter 3   Anaconda
Chapter 4   First Round

Part IV: Transition
Chapter 1   Transition
Chapter 2   Crossing the Bar
Chapter 3   The Hunt
Chapter 4   The Chase
Chapter 5   The Assault

Part V: Home front
Chapter 1   Home front
Chapter 2   Allegiances
Chapter 3   Preparing
Chapter 4   Search

Part V1: Expedition

Chapter 1   Expedition
Chapter 2   Refugees
Chapter 3   *Juanita*'s Woes
Chapter 4   Recovery
Chapter 5   Phoenix

Part VII: Consequences

Chapter 1   Spoils
Chapter 2   Retribution
Chapter 3   Exodus

List of Characters
Nautical Terms & Slang
Map
AMERICA's sail-plan and rig

The Yacht *America* in the Civil War

The yacht *America*, was once deliberately sunk by the Confederate Navy in an obscure Florida creek. She lay underwater for almost a week before her whereabouts was revealed by a sympathizer and she was salvaged by the Union Navy.

Not a shot was fired during the seven days it took to raise her, despite both sides being aware of each other's presence.

Partially due to the demeanor of the southern gentleman who lead the locally manned cavalry unit encircling the site. He declared it would be like shooting fish in a barrel, tantamount to murder. But he, and his fellow cavalry members, were aware their families, homesteads and the community of Welaka (the river of lakes) on the eastern bank of the St. Johns River, would be torched in retribution by an avenging force.

How did the world's most famous yacht, whose exploits garner the attention of sailors everywhere once every four years a century and a half later, end up scuttled in the brown, brackish Dunns Creek waters surrounding Rat Island, in the midst of the greatest conflict in the New World's history?

It's a tall yarn.

Author – Jack M D Owen

Part One

The Challenge

Chapter 1

AMERICA sets Forth

Flickering street gas-lights deepened shadows within the boatyard. They concealed the runaway boy and his black cat. Only the bass blast of a distant fog-horn downriver toward the mouth of the Hudson, and rumble of a steam tug-boat fighting the ebbing tide, broke the still of the night.

Sammy Taylor waited until all activity died aboard the sleek black-hulled schooner, after the last light was doused, before he dared sneak aboard to conceal himself in the forward sail locker. He and Bambino snuggled together under layers of cotton much softer than any of the sack-cloth bedding they had been used to.

It was a shame to soil them.

~~~

A faint glimmer of light pierced the forward hold and an unusual up-and-down twisting motion, at first pleasant but then uncomfortably nauseating, roused Sammy from his slumber. The bow of the yacht *America* lifted to the first waves of the Atlantic Ocean on the first day of her journey to the Isles of Wight off the English coast, and the race of her life at Cowes for the Hundred Sovereign Cup that summer of 1851.

Its historic significance was lost on Sammy, though. Along with the remnants of his last meal with the addition of green bile retched onto those fine cotton sails.

Bambino quickly adjusted, did his business in the bilge and returned with a plump, but slightly bloodied and mangled rat, as a gift. It triggered another round of dry-heaves from his teary-eyed, gasping young master. The pragmatic feline wasted no time consuming his trophy, cleaned, preened and slumbered.

A shushing sound of water sliding past the bow, the sound of boots on the deck above and Sammy's moans filled the compartment. An occasional shout, rattling and squeaking sounds from blocks and tackles protesting to a change of tack, followed by a shift favoring one side to the other with a constant sense of forward movement, was a novel experience.

The noise awoke Bambino. Following his natural inquisitive instincts, the cat set off to explore his new home.

~~~

Sammy woke abruptly when bright sunlight together with a gust of salt-laden air flooded into his hideaway.

An equally harsh stream of salty cuss words, followed by the strong hand grip from a bushy-faced sailor peering down at him, left him no resource but to clamber on deck.

"Stowaway. We've got ourselves a stowaway to feed to the sharks." The beard parted with a bellow.

"Where? Who? What?"

Men surrounded Sammy, feet barely touching the deck on his journey from the schooner bow past the dog-house toward the cockpit where the Master, Captain Richard Brown lit his first pipe of the day.

"Put him over the side, along with that damn cat," he pointed toward a writhing sack, secured by twine wrapped around its neck, jostling and flopping within the cockpit.

"No." Sammy screamed, wrenching free of his shirt to hurl himself protectively at the sack. Its violent movement stilled at the sound of his voice and embrace.

"Ah. Now we know where it came from. And who brought that bad-luck aboard."

"But Captain, sir. The boy's broke the curse. We're fourteen aboard now, not unlucky 13," piped up a portly figure that had emerged from below at the sound of the commotion on deck. The cook, balding head shiny with sweat from the galley, pointed a wooden spoon toward the intruders.

A chorus of agreement echoed his word.

"Lookit that." Sammy's captor pointed to welts on the skinny white back, cuts and bruises on his neck and face.

A ring of faces peered curiously down.

"That's enough. Get back to work. Me and the Mister will consider it," Brown waved his pipe forward, dismissing them. "Cookie, take the boy below. Set him to work. And his cat."

He prodded the sack gently with a boot, before turning his full attention back to the set of the sails, the fluttering leech, the angle of the tall masts, pitch of the bow, wind and wave direction. The smell of bacon wafted up from below, set his empty stomach to growling. It would not be long before those working guests, who had their sea-legs, would emerge from their cabins.

The cook retrieved the remnants of the shirt, the subdued sack and guided the boy below. That pale greenish-hued face faded to mere ashen, and a timorous smile of gratitude lifted Sammy's lips. *America*'s newest crew-member was born-again in that moment.

"What's your name, boy?"

"Sammy, Samuel Taylor, sir."

"I ain't a sir. I'm Cookie. Now the skipper, him with the pipe, he's a sir. And that there man leaning over the side, mebbe you didn't see him, he's the Second Mate, an' he's a sir, when he ain't being sick. Here boy, keep this yer bucket alongside – just in case. Put your shirt back on and wrap yerself in this apron. Dunno why though – it's cleaner than them there rags you'm wearing, if yer asks me."

Cookie rambled on while he rattled pots and pans around the tiny galley which seemed custom-made for his girth. A bucket of water and stool became Sammy's workplace to peel potatoes. Bambino purred on top of his former prison sack, tip of his tail twitching, ears pivoting to every new sound.

"Ah, bacon." A young voice called out followed by a

lanky youth with a stubble of peach-fuzz on his chin. His hand reached toward the draining rashers.

"Ouch."

"Wait your turn, Master Steers." Cookie rapped the knuckles none too gently, in a familiar ritual.

"But I'm fading away. Hello, what and who's this then? Shark bait?" George Steers II laughed, sucked his knuckles then pointed at the boy and cat, staring up at him.

"Never you mind. They's my helpers, not yorn. Get about yer business now. Them lamps needs filling, don't they? You'll hear the breakfast bell. You ain't deaf to that, are ya?"

Undaunted, bright eyed and quick as a red-squirrel, the youngster snatched a crisp rasher, waved it in salute, winked at Sammy and darted out of reach of Cookie's delayed swipe with the spoon.

Sammy smiled at the exchange when Cookie tut-tutted, then chuckled.

"He's a lad, that one. Slick as quicksilver with his hands and tongue. He could teach a snake how to wriggle out of a tight spot. Watch he don't lead you into any mischief, now. He's a master at it. I'm surprised his daddy's got any hair left. That's Mr. Steers, to us, eh. The brother of the man what designed her," his hands indicated the craft they were in. "He's the Mister George."

Sammy's hands and mind, fully occupied trying to absorb his new world, were lulled by the boat's motion more than disturbed as his body made the adjustment from land to sea. He was even able to nibble on a scrap of toasted bread crust, trimmed by Cookie's butcher-knife from the bacon sandwich he had prepared.

"When you've finished, take this up to the Captain." He poured amber ale into a pewter mug. "That's his. Don't drop it, or spill it, y'hear? And remember, one hand for yourself and one for the ship." Cookie prattled on, placed a cloth on a wooden tray before setting the food and drink upon it.

Sammy felt its heft, adjusted his hold and began a

staggered jig toward the cockpit.

"Don't look at the tray," Cookie cautioned. "Pick a point ahead and move the tray to stay level."

Determinedly, Sammy took another step, then again until his head poked into the daylight of the cockpit and the titled-horizon beyond. The cloth was damp, but not awash. The Master, 'Dick' Brown, normally captain and part-owner of the pilot boat *Mary Taylo*r out of Sandy Hook, scooped the tray out of his hand, setting it down in a secure nook before grasping his mug for a deep quaff.

"Ahhh. First of the day," he sighed. "Good job, boy. Don't tarry now. Off you go."

Sammy nodded, took a deep breath of the fresh air, then ducked below, smiling.

It was the first of many tasks and lessons he learned aboard the sleek two masted 170 ton vessel which spent the next three weeks swiftly slicing through the deep blue waters of the Atlantic between the continent of America and the port of Le Havre, France. There she would be tuned in preparation to a challenge issued to England's fastest yachts, in a race at the yachting center of Cowes on the Isle of Wight, before Queen Victoria and nobles of her kingdom.

Sammy was a quick study. Luckily, the resilient child made a swift recovery from *mal de mere*. Far sooner than the experienced second mate, together with the carpenter, who favored a few drops of brandy and water to solid food for the first few days.

Cookie, was also in charge of minor medical matters aboard *America*. His mixture of herbs for headaches and toothache, stop or go fluids depending on the bowl ailment, ointments and bandages for cuts and bruises also was pressed into service in his galley. Chicken soup embellishments, bacon and beef greases for cooking together with beer and wine flavoring were the special ingredients added to his meals which had made him first choice to man the galley.

One favorite, which Sammy peeled and diced carrots,

potatoes and onions for, was a Sunday Roast beef, and a New England recipe for Yorkshire pudding Cookie had picked up during his floating career. Sammy who, with his cat, had scavenged for scraps on the alleys and streets beyond the wharves lining the island of Manhattan, watched in wonderment at the raw vegetables being transformed into a feast.

The plate scrapings did not blunt the appetite or activities of Bambino, however. He periodically reappeared from sorties into hidey-holes beyond the reach of man, with a long-tailed furry trophy.

The aroma of fresh-baked bread had noses sniffing the air from the crew in her narrow bow to the cabins of her owners and officers 90-foot back at her stern. All hands messed at the same table, at different times during the different watches, day and night, during the 3,500 mile cruise. Sammy's name was not added to the ship's roster or log and he was not to expect any wage.

"You can either walk home," Captain Brown jerked his thumb toward the rolling white-topped waves racing along her hull, "or work your passage to our destination." His gruff pronouncement set the terms. However, he was the first to take the time to explain parts of the craft from port and starboard, fore and aft and the difference between lines, ropes, sheets and halyards to the confused landlubber.

Taking his lead, other crew members taught by example the variety of knots, fancy and practical, used aboard. And why the speed of the boat across the surface of the water, was called out in knots instead of miles per hour.

Curiosity drew him to the cluster surrounding the mate, holding in one hand a small sand-glass and chalk-board Sammy remembered from schooldays, with his other raised. When he chopped his hand downward the seaman leaning across the bulwarks, dropped the log he held. Swiftly he paid out the loosely coiled line, with knots in it, while the log skipped across the receding waves.

"Stop!"

The mate raised the emptied glass and his arm in unison. The calloused seaman's hand clasped the running line firmly, stopping any further escape. He wrapped a strand of spun wool loosely around the first knot he encountered, then carefully re-coiled the line until the log emerged level with his waist, to be hauled in inboard.

"Well?"

The old salt carefully counted along the dripping line until he reached his temporary woolen marker.

"A whisker over eleven knots, sir."

He had once erred when a disturbance interrupted his count. It cost him free time during the dog-watch make-and-mend which he had planned to use to darn his socks. Instead, while his mess-mates jeered him on, he spent that time practicing how to count correctly.

"That's the trick to it."

He held up the soggy strand of wool dripping before Sammy's curious face.

During slow periods and while Cookie applied odd-smelling unguents to Sammy's skinny frame to help heal bruises, welts, cuts and bite-marks, he relived his recent past.

"Mother and I were made homeless during the smallpox epidemic last year." Cookie nodded and spread the grease across narrow shoulders. "A tradesman took pity on us, we first thought, when the bailiff evicted us and we stood with our few belongings in the dusty road while former neighbors swept by, ignoring us." There was no bitterness in his telling. His story reflected what he had seen.

His choice of words, elocution and implied deference to his elders, distinguished Sammy from ragged mudlarks and wharf waifs scavenging through slime at low tide for any discarded salable object – living or dead.

Within days the entire crew from sail-maker to skipper, thence to the sailing syndicate who had conceived the notion of a yacht to challenge England's finest craft, knew Sammy's story.

Each time Cookie stopped by the scuttle-butt to replenish water and break away from his galley, he dispensed morsels of gossip about the boy. Soon, few were not aware of the family's financial loss together with social station. Of the kindly Swiss patisserie, widowed with a growing older son, who's offer of accommodation in exchange for assistance in the kitchen and shop, soon extended to unwanted amorous pressures.

"If she'd just given in, all would have been well,"Cookie shrugged to the nods of his mates. "But no. In frustration the cake-maker lashed out at the boy, and his son joined in. Course, that's why he's so handy in the galley, learned a trade, he did. And cleans a good pot and a plate too."

His mates laughed when he rubbed his belly and licked his lips. The boatswain's approach dispersed the lollygaggers. He asked what all the levity was, so the cook repeated and embellished the yarn, once more. The death of Sammy's mother, ruled accidental by the pastry-maker's family doctor when he so informed police, from a blow to the head, was attributed to a tumble down the stairs. Sammy's protests she was pushed, only brought a thrashing from the father and beating by the boy. He determined to escape with the cat that was constantly tormented by the older boy.

"He's no bigger than a pinch of salt," Cookie laughed. "But watch your step with that one. Before he stole away, he mixed handfuls of salt into the sugar bin. In the dim night light, preparing to bake, it was not noticed. Sammy and Bambino slipped away. They missed the fun when the sour-faced patrons would have called at the pastry-shop next day, to protest." Cookie chuckled.

The jape left the crew a tad leery of the cheerful, blossoming boy who eagerly soaked up all the stories and lessons they imparted during the three weeks he shipped with them.

"Captain, we'll need to fine tune and test our equipment and drills *tout de suite,* rapidly, when we reach Le Harvre," designer George Steers said at dinner while Sammy tended table. "Our racing sails must be inspected and tested, rigging tuned, masts adjusted, bottom inspected."

"Yes, but no scraping her bottom. That slick slime we've acquired will be like grease on a brick. However, we don't want any barnacle, critters or weed below the waterline to impede our progress," added his brother James. Both were listed as passengers but, together with young George, were available as extra hands if needed.

America's owners would meet them in France when they disembarked from a more luxurious transatlantic steamer from New York.

Chapter 2

A Challenge to the Best

In the beginning the new country of America struggled to survive within the untamed borders of its ever expanding world. Making a living drove man, beast and boat from dawn to dusk. Beset by enemies at every turn on land and sea, there was no time for luxury beyond the threshold of one's own domicile.

But in the space of one lifetime the trappings of wealth were apparent in the shape and size of homes, liveried carriages, pedigree of livestock and craftsmanship of vessels created for merchant princes. The era of the clipper ship, which raced China tea half way around the world to the gentry and drawing rooms of England, won the hearts of sailor and landlubber alike. In a world briefly free of the strain upon national treasuries to finance wars, the display of wealth and power evolved into the competitiveness created by fine horses and the sport of kings, plus that provided by luxurious yachts.

For the nation of seafarers, yachts became their nautical horses and the sea a race-track in the summer.

The Isle of Wight, the largest island in the English Channel, was comfortably within sight of the coast, with protection of the Royal Navy at Portsmouth and the busy waterways leading to the merchant seaport of Southampton. It was an ideal location for the British monarch to get away from the noise and summer smells of London.

The colorful cliffs with multicolored sand, verdant rolling hills and sheltered waters from the sometimes boisterous waters of the English Channel, suited Queen Victoria, Consort Prince Albert and her children. A highlight of the holiday was the annual August race around the island of some of the assembled yachts.

"But why would they do such a thing?" She asked her equerry, provided by the Royal Navy.

"It is the nature of sailors, Ma'am. Two boats cannot occupy the same sea pointed in the same direction, without competing to out-sail each other. Whether they be yacht, or barge."

"How very extraordinary. They're just like my boys," she confided to her lady-in-waiting. "I wonder how my son would react?"

Her eldest boy, Prince Albert Edward who would later become the Prince of Wales, never got the chance.

~~~

Principals of *America*'s investors, who opted to take a packet steamer across the Atlantic, joined the schooner and tuned her for the race which had begun to take on a life of its own. Far from the eyes of the normal shore-bound crowd, a groundswell of interest culled from sporting and society publications of the day, peculated from drawing room to scullery within the great homes of Britain, and her Continental rivals.

Her full suite of newly-cut and stitched cotton sails were bent on, exchanged, bundled below ready to be broken out and bent on again, depending on wind and water conditions. The French coastal waters of the English Channel presented similar conditions and challenges, away from prying eyes from all but the most ardent competitors.

While some gentlemen accompanied wives to the salons and milliners of Parisian salons, and selected wines fit to entertain Queen Victoria and her court, other members took *America* through her paces in the irascible waters lapping the shores of Le Havre.

Ships boy Sammy was pressed into service on deck too,

after a crewman miss-stepped into a knotted coil on deck just as the log-board went over the side. His yelp of alarm, which triggered the quick grasp of the old salt and the languid pace of *America* at that time, saved serious injury to his foot. It was enough to retire him from topside services, though.

During the three weeks of endless evolutions testing multitudinous combinations of sails, on all tacks, and weight shifts by relocating crew fore and aft, port and starboard, *America's* hollow wedge bow and lead-colored hull sliced easily over, rather than through Channel waters.

Local skippers of working schooners, comfortable aboard their bull-nosed plodding craft, watched in wonder, while calculating how many hours or days they could trim from coastal trips with such a hull. There would be loss of cargo space – but if they could beat their competition. Others forecast doom and catastrophe with the lightweight cotton fabric harnessing the power of the wind.

"There's no escape for the wind," one sage shook his head to another. "My friend Francoise, brother of the mayor, was a guest aboard. He said he could feel no wind on the billowing side of the sail. Mark my works. They won't last."

Captain Brown had launched a barrage of Anglo-Saxon words when he spotted the man Francoise standing in the lee of the mainsail holding a lighted cigar a tad too close to the flammable material. The Frenchman was so intent watching the smoke rise uninterrupted until it faded from sight high overhead to heed the words until a rough grip clasped him by the scruff of the neck, then wrenched the cigar from his hand prior to tossing it into their wake.

His friend sipped his absinth with a grimace of satisfaction, nodding his head in agreement.

And in truth, the debate below deck aboard *America* around the dining table echoed the issue.

"They were woven from the finest long-fiber Sea Island cotton produced in the south," designer George Steers argued with his brother James. His 17 year old son watched the conversation bounce back and forth across the dinner table like the newly introduced Goodyear tennis balls introduced to the garden game, a year earlier.

The sail-designer demonstrated with a scrap of cotton he carried with him to persuade skeptics, of its tensile strength.

"Pull that," he flipped the material across the table. *America*'s owners George Harkness, with William and Horatio Comstock also seated at the table, smiled. They had raised similar questions and partaken of the same demonstration.

"Don't fart, uncle!" The irrepressible George junior dodged a cuff from his father and retreated to the galley.

James strained with one, then both hands, to rip the material firmly anchored in his brother's grip. By the time his lips were tightly compressed in a bulging red face, many more crew-members had wandered below, on some pretext errand, to observe.

George looked at the audience. Unexpectedly he released his grip and his brother struggled to maintain his balance to avoid a tumble backwards.

"Put your faith in *America*, and the weft and woof of our God-given cotton," George addressed the crew.

"Yassah, massah." An unknown New England voice piped up in husky mimicry of a cotton-picking slave.

The laugh which followed drowned any retort the designer may have flung back. All were aware profits from raw materials, traded to the mercantile nation they were about to challenge on her home waters, had paid for the vessel underfoot.

"All well and good," the pragmatic Captain Brown said. "But if you gents sails don't work, we'll have *Mary Taylor*'s rough and ready work sails, standing by." He wrapped his knuckles on the wood table. Others followed suit on bulkhead, table or chair within reach. Some saw it as a good omen for the sails of the captain's working pilot ship out of Sandy Hook, also designed by Mister Steers, which had beaten *America* during trials, were also aboard. The combination of an innovative fast hull and proven traditional sails, were obvious, to them.

Sammy, washing dishes as quietly as he could manage in order to overhear the conversations, secretly hoped they would replace the cotton sails. He could still see, no matter how hard he scrubbed, the ghost of a stain from his night of shame when he first shipped aboard. No one else, except maybe the captain, seemed aware of it.

A fur body rubbed against his legs where Bambino's pleading eyes glared up from the deck.

"Oh, now you want to be my friend," Sammy teased. "It must be scraps time, eh?" He flicked water at the spot where the wily cat had stood seconds earlier.

Bambino combined a hiss with a purr from his new perch, on the fresh vinegar-scrubbed meat block. He had become a hammock-hopping companion to cat-lovers aboard, deftly avoiding cuffs and kicks from others not so benign, during their weeks at sea. An occasional headless rodent, not always appreciated, was presented in exchange for the more succulent scraps Sammy saved for him. There had been roast turkey, salt pork and beef, even tender veal in calf's jelly pie. A far cry from the fodder of the patisserie and his bullying son.

~~~

That far off night, when Bambino was being swung by his tail seconds before Sammy barged the bully to the ground – then ran – changed their lives.

For days they meandered streets and alleys avoiding two and four-legged predators teeming the wharfs, warehouses and yards where thievery was followed by swift punishment outside the laws of the land. They wandered further afield, both living on scraps, until they saw two rakish masts stretching high into the sky, seeming to beckon them toward the sleek leaden-hued hull with the gold eagle across her stern. While Bambino wet his fore-paw and preened, Sammy sheltered in the gloom of a toppled barrel beside a brewery, watching the comings and goings while *America,* the name on the ship's stern, was loaded with stores.

"Tomorrow I arise very early, scrub some of this muck off me, and see if I can't earn a coin or two – and a meal," Sammy told his furry companion.

That plan was thwarted when the drovers ceased deliveries, the laborers were paid off during the last rays of sunlight and one hailed a crew-member.

"May the wind be at your back and the seas as smooth as a baby's bum."

"Ha...we'll know this time tomorrow. We'll be far out to sea, away from this cess-pit city," the reply echoed around the stilled wharfs and off the warehouse walls. They waved in departure. One ducked below-deck, the other headed for a nearby tavern, Sammy guessed.

"Change of plan," Sammy confided to the purring fur ball curled in his lap. "Tomorrow we become sailors."

~ ~ ~

A month later they were in a new home and a new country. Sammy was as excited as all aboard *America,* and as exhausted from practice drill, replenishing stores, scraping, scrubbing, painting and polishing to present a pristine image to their competitors, Her Majesty Queen Victoria and all royal observers.

All hands were ordered on deck after the precious case of fine wine, fit for a Queen, was carefully passed hand to hand to the floor of the main cabin occupied by Commodore Stevens and his wife. There he concealed the rare wine from prying eyes. Unfortunately, the only other person who knew of the secret compartment was designer George Steers who really appreciated fine wine, as the commodore discovered to his chagrin, later.

Once *America* was 'ship-shape and Bristol fashion' as British sailors called a pristine ship with perfectly stowed cargo and stores, together with ships gear in tidy condition, *America* was ready to face her greatest challenge; the finest craft the Royal Yacht Club Squadron could produce. Catching the ebb tide and flow of the River Somme, she departed France to rousing cheers and waving flags from many ships who wished her well against France's traditional foe.

All eyes were strained north for the first sign of land during the 100-mile plus cruise across lumpy gray seas, through busy shipping lanes, toward the English coast. A darker line at the horizon eventually evolved from matching sea and sky to turn into green hills and multicolored cliffs as the island blockading the naval ships of Portsmouth and merchant vessels of Southampton appeared on the Solent.

A pilot steam launch guided her inshore to the lee side and sheltered waters of west Cowes. From the moment she hove in sight she fell under close scrutiny of the dozen ships assembled thus far. The yachts, some with owners belonging to several prestigious local clubs as well at the Royal Yacht Squadron, were curious but reluctant to meet the challenge of a 53 mile race around the island for a gaudy ornate silver chalice, and a hundred sovereigns.

For a while, no one would risk a race against *America* which, they espied closing to shore to rendezvous with the pilot, seemed to float across the waters rather than batter her way through them.

America's owners were afforded an affable welcome by the yacht club, encouraged to eat, drink and disclose as many secrets as their benign hosts could pry from them. George Steers proudly rattled of the statistical descriptions of *America*'s construction, types of wood, weight of ballast created to fit snugly between her ribs, with no risk of shifting. The rake of her masts; the foremost more than seventy-feet and the main more than one-hundred with her top-mast, gave her the appearance of forward movement even when she was moored.

Curious onlookers roughly measured the rake of her masts, holding a hand with thumb level with her waterline and forefinger, stretched without strain, followed the angle.

In a few days Her Majesty, Queen Victoria, monarch of England and her court would take up residence at Osborne House, East Cowes on the other side of the Medina River. Weather permitting, Her Majesty would board the royal yacht, the side-wheeler *Victoria and Albert* to observe 'The Queen's Cup' race from a vantage point at sea.

Now there had to be a race.

It came down to money.

Her Majesties loyal subjects could not be compelled to participate, despite the Royal Yacht Squadron courtesy temporary membership to several other yachtsmen, including their American cousins from the New World.

Within their own sphere, while competition was sometimes savage between social rivals, regattas were an insider affair. Members pooh-poohed the ideas of the upstart challengers, much as their company and delicious wines endeared the fellow yachtsmen to them, actually winning the race.

But they could.

Which could ruin reputations when HM expected them to be her Britannic champion..

In a cigar-fogged cabin, banker-yachtsman-founder of the New York Yacht Club, Commodore John Cox Stevens, called up those members of the syndicate to chip in a few dollars to sweeten the pot.

"Just how much molasses are you considering, dear friend?" George Schuyler tilted his wine glass toward the sweet amber rum favored by Stevens. The light jab raised a chuckle from his companions.

Stevens smiled back. Not always a sign of jollity.

"If we return without competing, we will be the laughing stock of all nations, no matter what the circumstances. You will find other ship-bottoms carrying our merchandise, our shipyards will sit idle, saw-mills fall silent, lumberjacks turning to poaching..."

"...all for the want of a nail," Stevens' brother Edwin

chimed in.

The atmosphere in the cabin took on a chill when the possible reality of the outcome sunk in.

"But what if we lose?" Schuyler asked.

"George, dear man. We'll be underdog heroes," the commodore raised his rum, a trifle unsteadily. "To challenge the British bulldog and show well, could increase our standing with fellow Americans, even more so than winning."

Smiles wreathed the faces of his companions. Losers could become winners, in the hearts of public opinion and fellow travelers, if they provided a good show. Based on reports trickling back aboard from the crew, who had become the toast of the town by the many visitors crammed into resort hotels and guest-houses encompassing the island, they had many supporters there, too.

Perhaps it was the frustrations they suffered, waiting for a proper invitation to show their mettle against reluctant participants more inclined to pose as fashionable salty gentlemen toffs. The British Isles, from pot-boy to peer, bore the air of superiority during that year of the Great Exhibition of Industry, hosted in London and showcased by the Prince Albert inspired Crystal Palace.

However, the image of 10,000 guineas proffered by NYYC's Commodore as prize for a competition against equals failed to root out a challenger or win over the most jaundiced gentlemen, despite their private opinion of the uppity Yanks.

Commodore Stevens could not return to New York without taking on the British. He finally agreed to participate against the odd-bag collection of yachts, big and small, competing for the traditional Queen's Sovereign Cup.

The date of August 22, 1851 marked a sea-change in yachting, world-wide.

The first international yachting race was, by default, the scheduled 'Queen's Cup' when no serious competitors responded to John Cox Stevens' challenge to enter his contest. He wanted an off-shore course against equals, schooner or cutter, with his offering of a 10,000 guinea prize to the winner. None accepted the challenge.

In a sporting gesture, America was invited as a guest to partake in a day-long haul around the Isle of Wight's 53-mile coastline, racing for the sovereign's cup.

The commodore, teeth gritted, graciously accepted

~~~

The jolly lark and socializing soon became serious business for most British yachtsmen.

Every movement and maneuver aboard *America*, above and below her waterline, was observed and analyzed by the experts.

One octogenarian national hero, with a wooden-leg, had 100 good reasons to discover or denounce a certain rumor circulating the club. It have would prove most embarrassing but for the quick action of Commodore Stevens. History records the old soldiers stoic comment to the Duke of Wellington at the Battle of Waterloo, when a French cannon-ball shattered his right leg during a cavalry charge.

"By God, sir, I've lost my leg!" Lord Uxbridge observed.

"By God, sir, so you have," Wellington replied.

The limb became a legend and its owner became the Marquis of Anglesey.

The battle-scarred soldier was also a formidable first-rank participating member of the squadron who watched *America* going through her paces from his own yacht, *Pearl*. She was easily overtaken by the Yank, as they called the challenger, under a sparse array of sails. Designer James Speer happened to be aboard the marquise's craft but none could pry the secret of her success from him.

"I think she has a little, what shall we say, Yankee ingenuity propelling her along," suggested one joker, polishing a well-circulated rumor tripping off the tongues of tipplers in many taverns lining the waterfront.

"Piffle!" The Marquis cloaked his comments in deference to the ladies aboard. "I'll lay you a hundred guineas you'll find no such thing."

There were none willing to match his offer. But, it had raised the curiosity of the wooden-legged warrior who, at the earliest opportunity, invited himself aboard *America* to see for himself. It was a very affable meeting. He and the commodore both savored a mellow glass of Madeira from the New Yorker's private stock obtained from the cellar of former British gentry. Their meanderings, with young Sammy proving a sturdy shoulder for the slightly wobbly older man to steady himself on, took them to *America*'s stern rail.

The marquis handed his glass to Sammy, lurched toward the stern rail and, balancing on his ample belly, craned his neck below the transom in an attempt to see any protrusion emerging from *America*'s stern.

"Oh, good God," The commodore dropped his glass which shattered on deck, to dart forward. "Seize him."

Putting his words into action, Stevens grabbed the jointed wooden leg with both hands firmly gripped the hinged ankle which leveled with his chest. Sammy swiftly placed the glass he carried, on deck, to clasp the old man's navy-blue uniform trouser-leg, trimmed with three gold-lace strips down the outer-seam.

All eyes, ashore and aboard boats of every description, focused on the trio tussling against gravity with *America*'s rail as a fulcrum to the marquis's world. A great cheer echoed across the water when the irascible grand old man, face wreathed in smiles, gained the quarterdeck again.

"Nothing to report, chaps," he bellowed. He waved his free hand to admirers while the New York Club commodore firmly clasped his other arm and swiftly steered the errant guest into the corral of America's rounded cockpit, away from any further temptation.

"You know, they're all convinced aboard the *Pearl* you've got a demmed secret engine, down there," his wooden leg thumped the oak-grating underfoot.

The commodore joined in the general laughter at such a preposterous concept, as the marquis considered, but the rumor persisted and reached fever pitch the day before the race was due when *America*'s keel shoe snagged an underwater obstruction, during a routine sailing exercise and tore it loose. The turbulence it created, close to the base of her rudder, required repair.

There was no time to return to Le Harvre dockyards and an underwater project in the tricky waters of Cowes could only be jury-rigged, and risky.

Ironically the Royal Navy, which had a long history of conflict with its American cousins, came to her rescue. The government dockyards at Portsmouth naval base, her shipwrights and workers, were put at their disposal.

"Its amazing how helpful the old-boy network has become," syndicate member and son of Alexander Hamilton, the late United States Secretary of the Treasurery, said. Colonel James Hamilton lifted an eyebrow when an aide from the admiral of the dockyard formally delivered a penned invitation to use the facilities.

"I wonder why?" Commodore Stevens smiled back.

Despite much rain the crowds of curious, and serious onlookers mobbed the area. There were those who studied *America*'s unobstructed underwater hull configuration busy with pens, pencils and sticks of charcoal to render her image from all viewpoints while she was exposed on the ways. English entrepreneurs were selling copies, complete with well-shod Victorians posed in the foreground. Other draftsmen meticulously noted length, breadth, depth and angles plus footnotes to their renderings.

"Awful lot of souvenir collectors, eh," Hamilton commented. Fellow members nodded.

All were aware of the designer's brother James Steers, who had stirred the rumor-pot a little, too. He had cautioned visitors aboard to stay away from a deck-hatch near *America's* stern, protected by a lashed-down canvas cover. No one, he smiled craftily, was allowed below deck, there. His nephew young George, who stayed aboard when his father and uncle were set ashore onto a train for Liverpool, and a packet-ship home before the historic race after the Commodore discovered the loss of his liquor, nodded silently in the shadows.

Dockyard workers and artificers milled around the broken sacrificial wood and shoe attached to *America's* keel, removed the damaged material and replaced it with time to spare before the rising tide crept up the slipways again. Many handshakes, and a few tankards of champagne clinked between the former foes before her lines were cast off and a steam tug towed her under bare poles back to Cowes.

A final huddle between the commodore and pilot, an Englishmen vetted by the no-nonsense Master, Captain Brown, some knocking on wood and a prayer for good winds, concluded a packed day.

Their future rested on the results of the next 24 hours.

Chapter 3

The Race

 For all the hullabaloo and anticipation it was hardly the most auspicious start for *America*.

 Morning mists shrouded the colorful cliffs and rugged coastline of the Isle of Wight, August 22, 1851. Long before dawn, thousands of visitors who had been pouring onto the island by steamer and wherry for days, stirred in beds crammed to capacity, even deckchairs on the headland and beaches, where they tried to sleep.

 Yachting, usually the preserve of the ruling class, had suddenly become a David and Goliath contest between Bother Jonathon and John Bull. 'Yankee Doodle' had won the revolution. Pride in Britain vied with a secret desire by many to see the fellow underdog, pull it off again, against the powerful upper class.

 The power wielded from wealth, by the non-titled American bankers, was basically ignored.

 Two rows of yachts, one of eight vessels the other of nine, lolled on slack water, pointed in all directions weighed in place by anchor and chain while odd currents and eddies swirled along hulls. Slowly, emerging from the moist air which dripped splotches of water onto decks from standing rigging and spars, hundreds of small craft from row-boats, sail to steam bobbed on the water in reaction to spectators moving about. The island had never seen anything like it. And the daylong race clockwise around the island would be within sight of all the spectators who shared the royal retreat, that summer.

Sammy poked his head into the raw air, bearing an enameled mug of coffee to Captain Brown puffing on his pipe, one booted foot on the slack anchor chain waiting for it to tense to the tug of the incoming tide.

"Big day today, sir." Sammy broke the reverie.

"Aye, boy. One you can tell stories about to your grand-children, I'll be bound." The master mariner cupped the mug in both work-calloused hands, talking through yellowed teeth clamped to the bow onto his pipe. His eyes moved from the eager face to the bow and latest irritant he had had to swallow, between master and owner.

A week earlier all hands had been turned to adding hardware to the forward mast and rigging for an additional sail, a flying jib, at the insistence of the commodore. The master had argued it would give *America* too much tug on the bow and a lee-helm which would pull her from a true forward course to put greater strain on rudder and helm. Despite his objections, backed by her designer who had built a sail-balanced boat, the flying jib with sails cut by the English Ratsey and spar supervised by George Speer, the additional hazard, to his mind, was added.

It lurked in the background.

Ships bells, paddle-wheels churning, echoed orders shouted across the still waters, plus the shudder of *America's* anchor-chain underfoot, returned his focus.

Brown shrugged, grimaced at the intake of coffee grouts in the last mouthful, and thumped his foot on the foredeck.

"'Eavo, 'eavo, 'eavo, lash-up and stow. Sun's burning yer eyes out, let's go, go, GO."

His bellow reached the deepest sleeper amongst the crew quartered forward, and owners snoozing in staterooms aft. The tide was turning, mist swirling in tentative breezes wafting in from the west. A patch of blue sky no bigger than the traditional Dutchman's britches, poked through gaps in the early-morning clouds.

Sammy darted from galley to crew and stateroom with plates of food, tea and coffee by the gallon. Master's orders, no beer tankards that morning. Bambino rubbed against stockinged and linen-clad legs, working crew and gentry with equal zeal for tidbits and petting. *America* rocked gently to the tug of tide and wakes of boats of all description of all shapes and sizes crisscrossing the surface of Cowes Roads between Southampton and the island.

Yachts of many sizes from schooners to cutters and yawls to the hefty 300-ton three-masted monster, *Brilliant,* were entered in the regatta. Ostensibly a splendid display of sleek craft bristling with polished brass and varnished bright-work under billowing white clouds of sails presenting an ocular feast fit for a Queen to review. However, no one present on the Isle of Wight that Friday, was unaware the nautical honor and prestige of a sea-going nation was at stake.

The 100 sovereign cup, wrought by London silversmiths R & S Gerard, was a silver filigreed frippery of no practical use of a price hardly sufficient to fill a gentleman's purse for an evening at the gaming tables. Of all the titled owners and pedigreed vessels entered from the finest

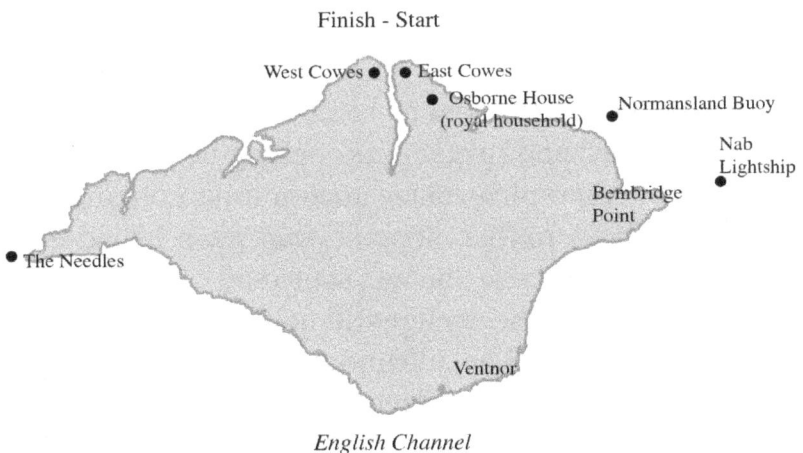

Finish - Start

West Cowes ● ● East Cowes
● Osborne House   Normansland Buoy
(royal household)   ●
                              Nab
                              Lightship
                     Bembridge   ●
                     Point

● The Needles

Ventnor

English Channel

yacht-clubs in the kingdom, *America* was the focus of all eyes and talk of many tongues. The nations of the world, brought to the head of the British Empire by the Great Expedition, had an international list of representatives watching and listening.

All attention swung between the boats, readying at anchor, and activities of the cannon crew near the Royal Squadron Clubhouse, awaiting the five-minute signal. The time ticked closer to the 10 a.m. start, sending hearts pounding, hands crossing in supplication and a surreptitious superstitious splash of liquor down to Davy Jones and the sea god Poseidon, just in case.

The whiplash cannon crack galvanized poised crews to slip cleated sheets to run sails aloft and take the strain on capstan bars; clicking each link of the anchor-chain aboard while Brown cautiously steered forward to break the anchor free at the 10 o'clock gun.

It was a maneuver *America*'s team had routinely completed without incident, dozens of times under the watchful eyes of England.

But a fickle cats-paw of wind from the west bollixed it up.

They could sense, rather than hear, spectators laugh.

In an instant the Master's planned departure: sails flapping, anchor-chain up-and-down with one tiny touch of the helm to fill the sails, run *America* forward, break the anchor from the mud below and sail into the Solent waters, was thwarted.

At the last moment an errant gust caught the new flying-jib, filled and tugged it propelling her hull forward to ride the rode, scraping coarse anchor links gouging into her sleek black bow. In that moment *America* rebelled against the wishes of her masters. She was set to sail on a tack of her choosing. Except, the anchor still held, forcing her across the wind, laying her on her side under the pressure.

Brown's bellow to slack sheets and lower sails as *America*'s bow swung back into the wind coincided with the sound of the Start cannon shot from shore, blanketed by a roar of spectators backed by tooting whistles from paddle-wheelers and whistles, rattles and trumpets from the fleet of little boats.

Sixteen boats got under way like a flock of doves soaring across the sea. *America* sat at anchor under a billowing cloud of dropped sails and a spaghetti-bowl of sheets, spars and running rigging flowing over guests, cabin-tops and her deck.

While cries of alarm arose from the honored guests invited aboard by the syndicate, Brown's bellows, honed in the treacherous Atlantic waters approaching the mouth of the River Hudson, steadied the writhing mass of men and sails into some semblance of order, again. Precious moments later while the fleet pulled away, under the eyes of nations of the world, *America* swiftly but calmly completed the maneuver with no problem except, she was left behind.

Last.

Fellow countrymen, who had wined and dined Commodore Stevens and the New York syndicate, were aghast. They had warned of the perils of holding their country up to ridicule before the crowned heads of Europe when their ridiculous experimental boat lost. Included was *New York Tribune* editor Horace Greeley, who was very fond of distributing advice. He had urged *America's* sponsors to withdraw from the contest. Above the sound of gnashing teeth and salty Anglo-Saxon comments a rumbling from massed spectators arose to a cheer when *America* caught the wind and, on a north-bound tack deep into the Solent, turned about on a lay-line to intercept the fleet leaders in clean air, clear of obstructive sight-seers bobbing about the waters.

~~~

The course to the first mark, Normanland Buoy off the north-east coast, would keep them on an east-south-east course for the first leg if the light westerly wind maintained. Most of the crew opted for the starboard rail, keeping the yacht's deck in the 10-knot breeze almost level.

To observers *America* appeared to float across the waves, barely slicing the water with her sharp bow. With fresh airs, uninterrupted by sails and steamers to windward she swiftly moved through the assembled fifteen craft who finally made up the fleet. Closing on boat after boat Brown took advantage of the cats-paws rippling the surface astern, cutting across it to blanket wind of craft to lee. Sails deflated when *America* aggressively pushed past, leaving the opponents wallowing powerless on the flooding tide, briefly carried toward the mainland.

"At this rate we should pass the leader in, say, 37-minutes, eh?" One of the guests chortled.

The Commodore's eyes squinted to slits. Captain Brown spat to lee and sailors within hearing scowled at the challenge to Sod's Law. At sea pleasure can change to pain in an instant.

America crept forward until there were only four hulls before them rounding the buoy. Ahead lay Nab Lightship offshore from the easternmost coast at Bembridge Point. Traditionally the course took a turn outside the lightship. But there was nothing in the rules forbidding otherwise.

"It's risky," the English pilot Robert Underwood had cautioned during the hours he and Brown discussed tactics and perils along the course. If *America* led closing on the turn, Brown was ready to follow tradition. But the laggardly beginning left little room for niceties.

All eyes swiveled from the craft heading toward the anchored ship to the east and Captain Brown head to head with the pilot. The commodore and his companions in the cockpit quieted their chatter too. Sammy paused in his duties, the surface of a fresh round of drinks slightly tilting with the motion of *America*, standing at the foot of steps leading on deck. The hatch framed the man who held the ship's destiny in his calloused grip.

Toward shore streaks of white water swirled across the green-gray waves flowing in under the influence of wind and tide pushing deep into the English Channel. A black throng of people covered the edge of cliffs overlooking the course hundreds of feet above surf which spent itself on sandy beaches below. Gusts of wind carried the salty tang of dried kelp, being covered by enveloping waters creeping up barnacle and shell-covered rocks, toward the approaching fleet.

The single mast of *Volante*, the lightest vessel with the greatest cloud of sail engulfing her, purposefully set a course for the lightship. As did *Aurora and Freak* in her wake.

"Can we do it?" Brown's eyes swiveled from shore to distant sails.

Dark clouds crowded the western horizon, winds direct from the Atlantic Ocean funneled between the channel shores when *America* poked her nose past the sheltering headland of the island. It should be her best point of sail. But her bow tugged, the helm fought Brown's grip so he braced booted feet against bright-work cockpit rails regardless of scuffs and scars which would mar her surface.

Brown clenched his teeth against the cold pipe-stem, the shoulder-muscles of a lifetime feeling the strain against the lee helm. His eyes met the commodore's, who nodded.

"Get the flying jib down, now," Brown called.

With alacrity the crew cast off sheets holding the sail to flap loudly to lee. Sammy, as the lightest crew, nimbly scrambled forward on her bowsprit to lash the sail securely down, as he had been taught. Heftier crew gathered armloads of cotton and smothered it under chest and belly, in a synchronized move which bunched the material neatly, despite pockets of wind wanting to billow it away.

Back on course from the slight jog into the wind, *America* resumed and surpassed her previous pace with lowered lee helm. Brown nodded his satisfaction. The commodore avoided eye contact, busy chatting with his companions pointing at the following fleet of racers they had left in their wake. The straggling sightseers dotted the watery horizon while smoke-belching steamships, paddles churning a wide white foaming path across the waves, struggled to keep them in view.

The rocks were being left behind them and the pounding of surf striking the beaches faded with every minute *America* added to the two hours it had taken her to take the lead.

Now she had to maintain it. There was only a brief interlude of sailing on a beam reach very far into the deeper sea before *America* would have to turn.

Gusting wind, striking towering cliffs, sent unsteady puffs in a flurry of confused eddies swirling unseen until they struck. Brown tacked back and forth across the increasingly powerful tide flooding through the English Channel. There was danger she would lose ground. While she sailed fast across the surface of the waves, the incoming tide threatened to push her back across that same seabed again. Their constant wind faded even as they criss-crossed, ready for the turn south of Ventnor which would take them westward to the prominent rock towers, known as The Needles, marking the western extremity of the island.

The flying-jib was raised again as every scrap of material, including the jocular waving of a silk-handkerchief by one of the wags well in his cups, sharing the commodore's bench. Brown scowled but clamped firmly onto his pipe and babied *America*'s helm, muttering softly to her, urging just a little extra if she'd please.

To spectators, including competitors, she appeared to be a puffy white cloud sailing serenely across an undulating emerald seascape emulating a rich seascape rendered by the popular artist JMW Turner. Below that scene of tranquility, tensions personal and physical, were at work.

A tilt of the deck, drag on the helm and splintering crack of wood forward of the bowsprit heralded a rogue gust of wind from nowhere. The cockpit became a pig-trough of sandwiches, fruits and cheeses sopping up spilled wine and beer mixed with cries of alarm and curses of blasphemy buried under Brown's bellowed command.

"Clear the deck."

The flying jib hung in a shambles, part of the jib-boom bounced across the waves tangled and suspended by twisted stays, swirling dangerously close to *America*'s hull. Blocks scythed through the air threatening rigging and any body-parts which got in the way. Part of the flying-jib stay snagged around the bowsprit bob-stay aiming the splintered spar toward *America*'s hull.

Sammy immediately scrambled swift as a monkey onto the swaying bowsprit dipping into the Atlantic driven swells pushed by wind and tide, while Brown held her head into the wind. Shouts, curses, flapping sails, chilled spray and the erratic plunges from sky to sea repeatedly dunked the boy.

His potato paring-knife, which he had taken to tucking into his belt like the real old salts, was clenched between his teeth pirate-fashion to use both hands and bare-feet to cling and swing under the bowsprit netting to slide down the bob-stay. Despite the pinching pain, he wedged his foot between chain and stay, looped one arm around the slick wood and sawed through layer after layer of manila fiber iron-taut from the foremast around the bob-stay to the bucking broken spar.

The shouts from the crew were blocked from his ears by frequent plunges underwater, flapping sails and choking fits gasping for air.

Without warning the resistance of the taut stay gave way to nothing when the knife sliced through the final strand. If his arm had not locked around the bob-stay he would have fallen from his perch, swept under the plunging bow and designated to the deep.

Unexpectedly he felt himself being hauled upward by the scruff of his jersey.

"Bath-time's over, kid."

The familiar taunting voice of young George Steers and his strong grip were welcome, for a change. Within seconds Sammy was retrieved from his perch, back on the swaying bow but with *America*'s solid foredeck underfoot. Cookie took charge, wrapping Bambino's hair covered and odoriferous sleeping blanket around his drenched and shivering former galley slave.

"Stupid ass, stupid ass."

He scolded in a litany, marching the boy below through a cockpit of well-oiled guests who greeted them with a smattering of applause for the impromptu entertainment.

Valuable minutes were lost, Brown noted. The fleet grew closer before *America* was fit to continue. The cutters *Aurora, Freak* and *Volante,* her three main contenders who had rounded the lightship, were still far behind. Another competitor, *Arrow,* had run onto rocks. It required a cruise-steamer to haul her free. He also noted the withdrawal of the yacht *Alarm* who opted to accompany her damaged sailing chum home, while paddle wheels of the impromptu tug churned full-speed ahead to catch the fleet.

While the tidal-race waters were chilly, based on the chattering teeth of Sammy, the August sun upon England's southern coast and constant tacking activity had *America*'s crew reeling. She edged forward toward St. Catherine's Point, the Isle of Wight's southern-most headland.

"Time to sit in the shade, lads. Once we slip around the corner. C'mon now, just a little more." Brown coaxed his crew. The gentlemen, sweltering in woolen suits and high-collared starched shirts edged toward the starboard seats in anticipation of the shade.

The British cutters were also struggling westward aiming for the silhouette of the raked masts shimmering against glistening waters glaring under the lowering sun. Time was ebbing, even if the tide was not. It was time to take a risk.

Closing toward the beach approaching the headland *Freak* and *Volante* chose to tack almost simultaneously, so close together *Freak* carried away the other cutter's jib-boom, narrowly avoided skewering a fore deck-man. The errant spar bounced off her assailant's shrouds then plunged into the waves. It took *Volante*'s sail with it, slewing her head across the waves. All aboard who had not secured a good grip staggered in a bizarre hornpipe before fetching up against something solid. Both vessels were out of the race.

By the time Sammy, dried off and floundering about in scavenged clothes, poked his head up from the hatch bearing a basket of fruit and sandwiches, the horizon aft was clear of all but one threatening sail.

~~~

America's distinctive but diminishing form was far ahead of the cutter *Aurora* gamely hanging in the race, passing their wounded companions with an exchange of compassionate cheers.

They were close enough to see spectators lining the headland waving the red, white and blue union-jack. A powerful back-eddy of wind redirected from the cliff-face puffed the cutter's sagging sails. The lightest vessel in the regatta dipped her bow into green water, tilted and left a wake bubbling astern.

"We can do it!" *Aurora's* skipper urged his flagging crew. "One more tack…"

The words were encouraging.

But their quarry slipped from sight beyond the headland on the horizon for a beam reach toward the Needles and the final turn toward the home stretch.

"It's our best point of sail, and the wind will shift with the sinking sun in our favor." The captain cajoled.

In an earlier era a rope's-end would have been the encouragement in his father's navy. The alternative was a tot of Jamaican rum ladled out by the captain's steward, following a smooth final tack, before the turn.

~~~

At the half-way mark *America* was in the lead.

While most of the spectators lining the shoreline awaiting a glimpse of the first sail to turn toward the Needles, concerned merchants, politicians, military men and members of the Royal Yacht Squadron were privy to the news ahead of the *hoi polli*. While swift communication by telegraphic means could transmit messages by Morse code between major cities, the resort island was not included. However, visual signals in the form of semaphore, common between ships of the Royal Navy, were available.

Certain admirals, staff officers and close friends with a vested interest in the results and odds bookmakers were offering, arranged for constant surveillance and updates over the course. The thrill of a gamble on the biggest race of the decade, totally illegal in Victorian England, was an irresistible lure to peasant and peer alike.

Prince Albert, the queen's German husband, was at the height of popularity following the successful response to the Great Exhibition and innovative hall built of steel and glass, quickly nick-named 'The Crystal Palace'. He urged his wife for the sake of commerce and diplomacy, to personally present the 100-sovereign race trophy stock item from the shelves of London jeweler Robert Gerrard. It had been bought and donated by the Marques of Anglesey the wooden-legged hero of Waterloo, to the Royal Yacht Squadron.

The antics of the sprightly octogenarian aboard the yacht *America*, seeking its secret source of power, had entertained Osborne House dinner guests on the eve of the race around the island, which highly amused Her Majesty.

A stream of messengers brought the latest race news, semaphored from coastal spotters manning sites established during Napoleon's reign of terror just scant years earlier. From the towers of her castle the waters of the Medina River were thronged with craft of every description and, Prince Albert noted, journalists from every nation in the world attending the Great Exhibition.

"One leisurely little jaunt in the comfort of your own yacht will allow your people to pay homage in an informal setting," he suggested cautiously, aware of her rigid attention to subscribed protocols. "Besides, it may take a little of the energy and steam out of the *kinder*, to be afloat beyond the castle grounds."

Members of the queen's household within hearing smiled. A few hours of relief from the rambunctious little royals ranging from babies to those on the cusp of adolescence, would be a blessing for all.

The side-wheel royal yacht steamer '*Victoria and Albert*' was moored in sheltered Medina River waters below the castle. The start and finish location would certainly be the focus of all attention, in a few hours. As dear Albert noted, it would be a pleasant way to conduct a social obligation and to be seen by her subjects in a significant historical moment.

"But, dearest, what if the American should win?"

"Why, we could challenge them to a rematch next year, and invite other nations to compete also. Rather a contest on the water, than a war on land, eh, eh?" The Prince Consort smiled.

"Oh dear. All these people, again." A regal wave toward the masses in many craft covering the waters below as far as the eye could see encompassed her broached sanctuary.

"Perhaps your majesty would enjoy a royal visit to the late colony to meet the challengers?" Albert teased. The mischievous prospect of the sovereign leaving her realm, raised a smile to her lips.

A discrete cough at the open drawing-room doors heralded the presence of the majordomo. An epauletted navy lieutenant, cocked hat tucked under his arm, white-gloved hand bearing an envelope, stood beside him.

"Admiral Pettigrew's equerry bears news of the race progress, ma'm."

"Albert." Her Majesty shied from being seen beyond immediate family and household wearing her pince-nez spectacles.

The Prince held out his hand for the envelope, flipped it open, glanced at its contents.

"The *America* has a good lead, approaching the Needles," he announced.

"They are first?" The question was posed to her trembling subject.

"Aye, er...yes, your majesty."

Albert smiled.

"And who is second?"

"Uhm...There is no second!" The words blurted out.

"Very good. Thank you." The Prince said.

Albert's swift dismissal prevented an interminable discussion and further embarrassment. At his leisure he would explain the nuances of yacht racing to dear Drina. But before the naval officer left the building, the household grapevine passed the morsel of gossip upstairs and downstairs through the ladies chambermaids.

~~~

America's crew stood by to make the final tack onto a beam reach. Her starboard rail tilted close to the sea's surface on a beam reach under a steady south-south-westerly wind. Far ahead to the west, lit by the late afternoon sun, the distinctive outcrop of rocks thrust upright from the shimmering waters like Poseidon's fingers reaching to grasp them.

And, a well-handled cutter perhaps two miles ahead of them.

"Where in the world did that come from?" the Commodore cried, echoing the question everyone wondered.

"Ha! A little spectator competition looking for a race." Brown snapped closed his brass and leather pocket spyglass. He glanced at the relaxing crew. "Don't get too comfortable, lads. What say we take on the Limey up ahead?"

With no competition in view behind the receding St. Catherine's headland, the only other vessels sharing their water were steamships rolling on the western waves. The competitive spirit of 'boys with boats' lay just below the surface of *America*'s old salts. They rallied from the sapping sea air, sun and creeping fatigue of their long day to the friendly challenge.

Aboard the 40-ton cutter *Wildfire* from the Royal Cork Club, its owner smiled with satisfaction.

Earlier, while the rest of the assembled spectator yachts pursued the regatta turmoil, he and his crew took a leisurely cruise westward. By taking the opposite course he planned to intercept, and accompany, the leading vessels on the homeward stretch.

No one anticipated the impromptu private race within a race which ensued.

It took an hour, much tweaking of sails and sheets, on both craft, for *America* to inch forward until a fortuitous gust struck her windward position, propelling her forward level then past *Wildfire*; close enough for the American schooner to take the wind out of her competitor's sails. An exchange of cheers and good-natured jeers, plus a doffing of hats by their respective owners, accompanied the maneuver.

"That could have been our last good gust," Brown noted.

He glanced astern, beyond *Wildfire* in his wake, where the familiar sails of *Aurora* had appeared beyond the steamships.

Drawing closer to the Needles, the Channel's late afternoon wind lessened to a breeze, losing some of its punch. The seas settled into a lulling gentle roll, no whitecaps to be seen.

Without the cocky little cutter to chase nothing lay ahead of them but the hypnotic lure of the pillars of rock rising.

The three cheese-wedge-shaped white slabs of chalk at the western tip of the island, lacked the distinctive needle-shaped tapering pillar of rock which towered 100-feet high between the second and third matching monoliths. Its soft base, eroded by countless storms and tides ranging up to ten-feet between high and low, collapsed under its own weight, the previous century.

"Give it a wide berth," the pilot advised. "It's tricky, all those gaps between the rocks, and currents from the Solent and Channel crossing each other. They ought to put a lighthouse there."

Brown nodded. He heeded the advice, picking ruffled patches of water from fluky winds rippling the surface of the sea. Slowly the rock profiles shifted from side to full on where the Needles appeared to move to stand one behind the other, before their north-face became exposed.

A final glance behind and, even without his spyglass, he could see *Aurora* had gained before they completed *America*'s turn to a north-east course with the air on his back.

Dropping winds accompanied the drooping sun. Far ahead the final horizon was black with hulls of all shapes and sizes. Most were topped by white or red canvas sails. Then there were smudges of smoke from steamers marking the beginning of the end of their quest for the Queen's Cup.

America was on her slowest point of sail with the wind astern, despite the vast array of fine cotton sails outspread like the wings of a dove landing into the wind. Her sails were spread out on either side, wing and wing. A following breeze was tricky. It held the possibility of a fluky gust catching the edge of a sail to send her boom scything across the deck, in an uncontrolled gybe.

"Stay awake boys. It's ours to lose. Hold your positions."

The crew, syndicate members and guests, were distributed evenly so she sailed upright. Any tilt, at the wrong moment, could trigger a series of reactions tumbling faster than a row of tipped dominoes. The tension during the final leg limited conversation to whispers. No laughter. Plenty of glances astern where the lighter-hulled *Aurora*'s bow seemed to grow larger by the minute, inching forward toward them.

It was long past supper, an evening drizzle drifted in with the sea breeze once they fought free of the lee of the islands cliffs. Sammy's light-weight figure scampered from galley to deck with little snacks, fruits and sweets composed by Cookie which could be eaten by fingers alone. There would be time later for grog and a full meal to celebrate, or mourn, their fate.

Closing toward the finish line the distinctive profiles of the queen's yacht *Victoria and Albert'* and auxiliary *Fairy* chugged through and ahead of the spectator fleet, eager also to become part of the grand finale.

Sunset lost its glow to the onset of a soft twilight. Faintly the sounds of ships bells echoed the sound of *America*'s eight-bells striking to mark the end of the last dog-watch.

When the royal representative of England drew level, Commodore Steven's ordered *America*'s ensign dipped and all on deck to doff hats. The cheers and clapping of nearby spectators who had enthusiastically welcomed the Yanks, despite the likelihood of a yachting loss for Britannia, swelled in volume.

The Commodore, a pragmatist of the first order, dabbed at a tear.

Her majesty and Prince Albert, smiled.

Aurora's blunt bow-wave could be seen just minutes behind. She seemed to be hauling a steady wind with her. The eyes and bodies of all sailors on both boats strained forward toward the finish line as though that would bring it closer to them.

The royal yachts slowed, turned and followed.

Less regal was the *frrraap* of Bambino's fart.

"Oh my Lord. Get that cat out of here," a gentleman raised a rose-scented handkerchief to his nose.

"You asked for a good gust, aye." Brown's droll comment broke the tension. Others, up-wind, also chuckled. Even the Commodore smiled watching Sammy scoop the odoriferous cat to safety.

Boats crowded in, leaving a narrow path free ahead, during the final moments.

Somewhere the sounds of '*Yankee Doodle*' drifted from the deck of a steamer.

A sea of red, white and blue fluttering cloth representing the Union Jack and newly created 31-star flag of America, waved like poppies in a field.

Just yards away the invisible line between two points marked the finish.

The crack of a cannon, at 8.37 P.M that August 22, 1851, was barely heard above the commotion when her original bowsprit crossed the line.

America, a scant eight-minutes ahead of all other ships, was first.

~~~

Politics, never far away from the social ladder, wrested the presentation of the cup suggested by Prince Albert out of the Queen's hands back to the Royal Yacht Squadron. Undaunted, the seasoned royal campaigner who had survived trial by taunts, cartoons and accusations by opponents of encouraging 'alien' terrorists to the land of Albion, via the Great Exhibition, suggested a benign alternative.

A note was received aboard *America* inviting the Commodore and crew to anchor off Osborne House following tea, next day, to receive a visit from the royal couple and court.

Meant as a compliment, it galvanized the spent crew into creatures reminiscent of whirling dervishes, dusting, scrubbing, polishing every reachable inch of the world's fastest sailboat.

Bambino was chased stem to stern, bilge to masthead by zealous *America* nationals and at least one make-up crew, in the whirl of activity. Sammy's hands wrinkled under the caustic soda soaking pots, pans and cutlery then stiffened from gobs of beeswax spread rubbed and polished on all wood furnishing. Including pantry shelves where sacks of grain, bags of potatoes and the newfangled canned meats and vegetables were housed. The galley sparkled, he told Cookie, just like the great Crystal Palace he had seen in the city of London.

There was barely room for *America* to be towed through a fleet of bobbing boats, up river to drop the hook in sight of the royal residence at the designated location.

The royal barge, its household flag languidly floating in the breeze, approached, took a complete turn around *America* to observe every aspect, and pulled alongside the port gangway to allow Queen Victoria to ascend. The young queen, in her thirties and barely into the second decade of her reign, graciously accepted the hand offered by the Commodore to step down into *America*'s cockpit.

"What a pretty boat. My compliments, sir, on its form and function."

"Thank you, your majesty – ma'am." Commodore Stevens adjusted his form of address as advised earlier by a royal.

"You are the host, sir, and as such your guest will defer to you." Then she cautioned. "However, please do not forget, you are hosting the Queen of England."

No one aboard that day was ever likely to forget it. Although Captain Brown, possessively proud of his command did caution the Prince Consort to wipe his feet on the rug, before descending into the main cabin. He caught the startled glance on the younger man's face.

"Oh, I know full well who you are, sir," Brown quickly noted. "But, you still have to wipe your feet."

Below the Queen explored and exclaimed while being led through every space from cabin to crew-quarters, to bilges and the in-place custom-fitted ballast casting, to the galley and pantry.

"Oh, my. How wonderful." She withdrew a lace-gloved finger from swiping a shelf in the pantry. No dust marred its delicate texture, which she displayed to the pristine Prince. Her eyes swept the faces of those assembled about her and noted the blushing boy.

"Well done, young man." Her eyes twinkled, knowing she had picked the right person for the compliment.

Sammy smiled his widest smile, ever.

~~~

The eight-day wonder ebbed with the tide of events elsewhere in the world.

The Royal Household retreated from the heat of southern England. The Queen preferred the grounds of Windsor Castle and the country banks of the meandering River Thames, to the cloistered air of Buckingham Palace within the confines of noisy, smelly London. Prince Albert had designs on a cooler, more isolated location further north in the Scottish grounds of Balmoral, Aberdeenshire.

America's impact on British shipping, both mercantile and pleasure, was already having an effect. Details of drawings and sketches, even images captured on chemically-treated glass plates in experimental photography tests, were studied by maritime architects and builders. Some applied the knowledge to reconfigure sail-plans and rigging. Others experimented with the lighter cotton sails. A trickle of trade and business accommodations developed between members of the New York Yacht Club and the Royal Yacht Squadron.

Commodore Stevens and his cohorts were well pleased with the experiment which had brought fame, if not fortune, to the enterprise. It may not have matched the industrial and mechanical abilities displayed by their host country at the Great Exhibition, but it amplified the inventive nature of the New World. The old guard aristocracy, which had fought Prince Albert on resisting sharing their knowledge with the people, awoke to the potential impact such an innovative new country could have on their *status quo*.

The NYYC partners decided to liquidate their financial investment, pocket the goodwill, the prize cup and any profits realized from the sale of *America*. They would depart Europe by steamer with tickets already purchased, and arrange for her crew to follow, except a caretaker, the cat and Sammy.

"Oh no sir, that ain't right," Cookie's high whine could be heard below and on deck when Captain Brown relayed the orders.

"What can I do about it? The boy's a stowaway, by rights he should be in the brig – if we had one." Brown huffed back. "He's lucky Mr. Stevens don't set him ashore to fend for hisself."

"Well, you can tell that mister Stevens if it hadn't been for young Sammy, here, we'd 'ave had a great hole in the bow from that there jib-spar bouncing around all broke and sharp," Cookie snarled back.

"What's going on here?" The Commodore's cabin door opened. He had obviously heard every word through the louvered door panels.

Sammy, the subject of all the wrath and emotion of the next few minutes, busied himself polishing silverware while Bambino lounged nearby, grooming.

"We need somebody we can trust to stay aboard, and watch the watch."

"He's just a child."

"I'd put him to work aboard *Marie*," Captain Brown volunteered his Sandy Hook pilot schooner.

"I am not accustomed to discussing these domestic matters with staff," the commodore bristled.

"And I don't take no shit from nobody," Brown bellowed back. The weeks of tension, muddled-headed decisions, plus the treatment of his friend George Steers, designer of both *Maria* and *America* vented with the force of a steam-boat whistle.

No one aboard paid much attention to their tasks at hand while the drama between foredeck and quarterdeck played out below. The remaining members of the syndicate still aboard, tuned in with equal relish, ears straining but safely out of sight behind closed cabin-doors. Cookie watched the heavyweights with the enthusiasm of a spectator to the newly popularized lawn-tennis contests.

"I say, chaps, package from Her Majesty." An equerry from the royal household dared to poke his head into the seething cauldron of spiteful words flooding the cabin.

With a physical effort of restraint, Commodore Stevens forced his lips from a snarl into a smile before moving to the foot of the companionway steps.

"May I help you?"

"G'morning sir. A little going-away gift. For the captain," he swiftly added before the Commodore's grasping hand could rip the wrapping from the small package.

The smile remained firmly in place, but the glint in Commodore Stevens' eyes was diamond-hard.

"Here, Captain Brown. We have both been blessed. Our country with the Queen's Cup and you..."

Brown's large textured hands swiftly exposed the black-velvet hinged box and a card engraved with the royal coat of arms, inscribed in a copperplate hand.

He squinted, holding it at arm's-length in the light beaming down from the open hatch.

"Well, read it man." A testy urging from the commodore.

We trust you will keep this memento
as clean as you keep the America

Brown's voice trembled with unexpected emotion. His eyes beheld a gold pocket compass residing in the gift-box.

"Thank you, Sammy." He switched his glance from the gift to the waif whose bees-waxed shelves had elicited the royal accolade which encompassed *America* and all who sailed upon her.

Brown turned back to the Commodore. "Now sir, about this boy's future.

Their conversation, which for weeks had focused on their future in royal England reverted to the more rural land of their birth, its present and future.

Part II

Florida

Chapter 1

Wilderness

Thousand of miles south west, across the wild Atlantic Ocean whose breezes had swept *America* to victory, the fickle winds and waters combined into the memorable hurricane of 1851 which battered the Florida peninsular, an appendix to the underbelly of the New World.

"Sink the boats in the shallows, take the horses to the high pasture and douse all fires." New Florida plantation pioneer, former cavalryman in the recent Third Seminole War, the 22-year-old 'Colonel' Winston John Thomas Stephens, rattled off orders.

Burrel Stephens, his black foreman, had alerted him something was 'in the air'. Birds whirled excitedly, worms emerged from the damp ground to wriggle away from the banks of the St. Johns River, and menacing thunderclouds westward were lit by green lightening. No fish had been caught in the shallows.

Fishermen told of schools of mullet moving to the deepest sink-holes in the lakes. It would take weeks for the news to reach those frontier families, but sand sharks moved off-shore from bars and reefs all along more than a thousand miles Florida's coastline days before what became known as the 'Great Middle Florida Hurricane of 1851', arrived.

The birthing of Welaka, the community known to the native tribes who had hunted and fished the land as the 'river of lakes', occurred during a powerful display of nature's power. Tide flooded land, winds of more than 120 miles an hour mixed with a combination of funnel-clouds, plus a deluge from the sky which had all who could read clutching their Bibles and citing Noah's Ark and the end of the world.

It was a scene far removed from the glittering crystal and silverware, pomp and circumstance of the yachting fraternity of England's Isle of Wight. But its role in the demise and rebirth of *America,* the world's fastest sailboat, began that summer.

The site of destiny housed a mixed bag of escaped slaves, indentured servants, mixed Indians, even pirates, who eked out a living on Rat Island. It was but one of hundreds of clumps of forested sandbars dotting the shore and lakes of the north-flowing St. Johns River. The somnolent brown and brackish waters meandered more than 300 miles from marshland deep south in Florida to flow northward until it met the eastern shore break in the sand-barrier to the Atlantic Ocean at Cowford, which later became Jacksonville.

That summer the daily downpours multiplied in intensity. Even the vermin which gave the island its name, began to scamper and swim toward higher ground on the mainland formed by a primeval ridge of shells, stones and sand which ran half-way down the state a dozen miles inland, parallel to the barrier island coast. The site where bison crossed in an earlier era, which became Buffalo Bluff, overlooked the lazy tidal river for several miles. The narrow shallows churned and frothed under the stream of cloven-footed creatures fleeing inland from unknown danger. A few Florida natives, descendants from vast tribes of Timucua who once occupied and tilled the land before Spanish conquistadors and other European explorers brought disease to the land, read the animal instincts and melted into the hinterland, too.

Winston and his brothers had no choice but to protect their family, slaves, livestock, homes and plantations out of which they wrested a living from the semi-tropical land. They were the latest of white settlers of many nations staking a claim on the land. This time, acquired by strong arm force of Andrew Jackson, five-million dollars and a treaty with Spain, southern settlers determined to stay.

A new slave state was born.

Their part of Florida, in many sections cleared of scrub pine for orange groves and cotton fields, had rolling hills visually reminiscent of northern states. Hardwood hummocks of evergreen vegetation housed good and bad plants for man and beast. They were like an oasis in a dessert. It was unlike the flat swamp-lands further south, closer to the great Lake Okeechobee whose waters flowed into the dense grasslands known as the Everglades.

An abundance of water was life and death for all, animal and human. It provided the first passages for migratory creatures and a liquid highway to transport people and products between the few settlements established in the state first explored and built upon by Ponce de Leon following Spain's claim to the new world of America four centuries earlier. Natives traveled and traded by canoe chipped and burned from abundant pine felled in the vast forested lands. Boats of every description powered by paddle, oar, sail and steam plied the waters from the St. John's source from marsh to stream, lake and river. It also powered the grist mills which ground corn into grits and flour which sustained both slave and settler.

The Stephens' properties supported two of the three brothers who migrated from lands earlier generations owned near Oglethorpe County, Georgia, before the 1776 war of Independence as they called it or, the American Revolution as King George III and his ministers referred to as the Colonial rebellion.

~~~

Distant rumblings and fiery flashes lighting the sky beyond the horizon foretold something more powerful than customary afternoon thunderstorms with torrential downpours for an hour or so, followed by suffocating heat from steam rising to reach the returned sunlight. The breathless twilight quickly overtook spectacular sunsets signaling the buzzing of a myriad insects and return of clouds of mosquitoes buzzing above the diminutive, but no less painful, bites of no-seeums.

"Have the children convey our dry goods to the hole-in-the wall,"Winston ordered. "And no skylarking, understand."

The last was aimed more toward Burrel's common-law twins, Moses and Joseph. They giggled. Though only three years old (Moses by 12-minutes more so) they, like everyone else, had tasks to tend. Burrel nodded and grinned, touching the rim of his plaited palmetto-frond hat. He and master Winston were not so old they could forget the pranks they pulled as tots back on the South Carolina plantation of his sire. He blessed the Lord he, his woman and children stayed together in Winston's inheritance and the family's relocation to Florida.

A cleft in the limestone a stone's throw from the outdoor kitchen presented the craggy face of a bluff which sheltered the house from the predictable boisterous nor'easter winds of winter. Temperatures could nip orange blossoms and put a cobweb skein of ice between blueberry bushes, some nights. A cave, judging by the scat maybe of a black-bear den decades earlier, provided a cool larder in summer. Burrel built a rude boarded door to keep scavengers at bay. A ramp across the rugged ground made access easier for boxes and barrels to be hauled the five feet up the slope to its entrance.

The land they leased and owned, on the eastern bank of the river, was half a day away from the nearest city of Palatka and the deep-water docks where supply steamers disgorged their goods, and loaded cotton and citrus to ship to the seaport or railway spur. They were on their own, hurricane or not.

"You boys, bring me some eggs, and be careful you don't scramble 'em, y'hear." Maryanne's husky voice carried from the kitchen. The world might be coming to an end tomorrow, but hungry bellies needed to be fed, first. The

'Colonel', as Winston was commonly addressed, exchanged looks with Burrel..

"Yes, momma."

The twins chorused in unison and skipped away. Even at their age they knew who was really in charge.

Winston sighed.

"When she's done with them..."

Burrel nodded. He watched his blood brother stride off toward the house where the widow Stephens and her youngest sons were busy preparing for the storms to come. They all knew, Momma really ruled the roost, despite their low social ranking.

The Florida peninsular attached to the greater continental shoreline of North America's coast divided the Atlantic Ocean from the Gulf of Mexico. Less than 100 miles separated its southern tip from a beaded-string of foreign islands and atolls scattered through the Caribbean basin, from the British-held Bahama Islands to a kaleidoscope of national flags from Spanish Cuba to the Dutch isle of Curaco.

The Stephens family were following in the footsteps of many who had sought riches from the picturesque lush greenery which fringed the 500-mile-long land of white-sand beaches and aquamarine waters lapping its shores. The low-lying land, less than the height of a man above sea-level for the most part, was pocked with lakes, aquifer springs, sink-holes, marshes and rivers.

Combinations of high winds and high tides could batter through shallow barrier reefs of sand, to inundate the terrain far inland. Inlets appeared and disappeared from early charts making any voyage along coastal waters, hazardous.

Inhabitants of the clear waters cast shadows on the sand and reefs below, sometimes leaping clear out of the water plunging and racing in the bow-wave of a boat, or frothing the surface in a school of jacks or mullets fleeing predators. Ashore, wild fruits grew in abundance, if one knew the harmless variety which could sustain life, in season. For, while it was more subtle than northern climes with its marked stark winters and burned-grass summers, Florida transitioned more gradually within its verdant face.

Hurricane season when wild winds spawned in the southern seas of the Caribbean spun northward, or devil winds born in the sands of Africa thousands of miles to the east blasted a course across the Atlantic, added to the perils of the summer season and its life-giving downpours.

Winston watched his own and leased slaves secure bales of cotton under hemp fishing-nets secured to tree-stumps still in the ground from the latest on-going ground clearance project. Soon, new citrus crops, yellow grape-fruits bigger than a man's fist, would be planted. They grew in clusters on the branches, like grapes. Unlike the oranges strung along thorny branches which fought and scratched against the scarred black-arms of the pickers.

The few settlers, including the Bryant family, biggest land-holder and founder of the newest occupants of Welaka, had invested their lives, fortunes and families in the land. Like many before them and generations after, they were mostly land-rich and cash-poor. Weather could make or break them.

In the summer of 1851, far away in the slave-free New England state of Connecticut, the seeds of a literary catalyst were germinating in the mind of a woman who, many years later delighted to soak in Welaka's sulfur springs. The abolitionist words of Harriet Beecher Stowe were being read serially at first, then in the story-book form of Uncle *Tom's Cabin*. The story captured the minds and motives of anti-slave activists, world-wide. It was a spark which fell onto kindling waiting to be fanned into an inferno by abolitionists, to cleanse the New World of its evil past, as they saw it.

But that faded into the immediacy of surviving the next few hours, or days, while nature's most powerful storm began to send bands of rain in ever-increasing intensity with winds accelerating above a hundred miles an hour.

All along the river banks preparations were made when

the word reached isolated homestead, plantations and communities by the gossip grapevine, carried by riders and boatmen, of a big storm brewing.

James Bryant, the patriarch of Welaka's settlement on the east side of the river, arrived unexpectedly in his *Juanita,* the steam-launch he had transported his family in from Jacksonville. That 20-foot open boat, with a canvas awning was towed at a steady10 knots for the first 60-miles by the paddle-wheeler *Florida* to Palatka. It was a big adventure for his two youngest children, 10-year-old Octavia (Tivie) and her 12 year old brother, Davies. They would be joining their extended family when they reached the land and house their daddy owned. But, most of all, they would have him all to themselves forever – or until they reached their destination.

"Oh, oh, Swep, trouble," Winston muttered to his brother Swepston upon hearing the steady thump-thump of the approaching launch *Juanita*. Swep nodded, moved along the dock to a piling to take a spring-line.

The Boston lawyer, merchant and editor could have been attending a grand-ball. Judging by his dress-coat, cravat and top-hat, hands resting on a silver-topped ebony cane with his equally formally-dressed children seated demurely on either side of him. The *Juanita'* skipper hefted a line ashore while a boy leaped to take a turn of the line around a dock-piling.

"Morning to you, Colonel," Bryant tipped his topper.

"And to you, sir," Winston touched the wide-brim of his woven hat. The 'Lord of the Manor' as most referred to the Bostonian, grimaced a tight smile. The little boy waved and the doll-like raven-haired girl blushed and coyly glanced toward him with dark eyes through heavy lashes.

In that moment the seasoned soldier, plantation-owner and man of action, succumbed to a force he had never experienced before.

Love.

He shrugged it off as an unseemly and unlikely

situation. But all the while he and Mister Bryant discussed the threatening situation, what preparations had been made and were still to do, Winston's eyes traveled to the children laughing and poking with a stick at fish rising to the surface to snatch crumbs from the picnic-cake they consumed.

That encounter played and replayed in Winston's mind for weeks, months and years to come before his desires were fulfilled.

Chapter 2

Schism

In the beginning, the English-speaking world of America held together in the new world against animal, human and climate peril with a shared nationality and a superiority of numbers, against foreigners.

That changed during the pioneering years of struggle, success and a sense of independence from their mother-country. It was something held in common by many subservient new world inhabitants until the day in 1775 when British citizens and others, miles away from the eyes of King George III's ministers, rebelled.

Three wars later in, less than a century after the United States of America won its independence, an internecine squabble pitching family against family; brothers, sisters, fathers and mothers against each other, a fresh conflict threatened their unity. It was a schism between the slave-holding agricultural south against the slave-free industrial north which no amount of talking could breech.

Plantation owners along the banks of the St. Johns River, and Palatka resident William Dunn Moseley, Florida's first state Governor following the change from a Territory in 1845 were gravely concerned. The state, roughly the size of England, Scotland and Wales combined, was mostly occupied within the northern section, where it shared a border with Georgia and Alabama, from the Gulf of Mexico to the Atlantic Ocean. It held but a handful of white population. Black field-hands who hoed, hewed, picked and packed the product raised on the arable land, vastly outnumbered them. Export, to northerners who relished summer foodstuff shipped by steamer and train during bleak winters of root vegetables; and cotton mills in England's murky Manchester who turned snow-white raw cotton puffs into fine cloth, was their lifeline

And slave-labor was its backbone.

Seven years had flowed by since Winston first glimpsed Octavia. He had fought in a war, the third attempt to rid Florida from the Seminole Indians, the Creek, Miskoee and slave runaways who roamed and raided from the depths of its wilderness. Winston's service in the Third Seminal War militia, took him deep into the tangled undergrowth which sheltered desperate armed men, along with all manner of known and legendary, creatures.

The ears of sentries would twitch to pick-up campfire gossip of enormous snakes which could consume an alligator, or swamp-men with splayed webbed-feet like a duck to cross the swamps, who craved human flesh. Mostly they fought swarms of mosquitoes that stung every inch of exposed skin before sucking blood so even the natural body-functions requiring some privacy, became a hazardous duty to perform.

Days after the 1859 incendiary action of abolitionist John Brown at Harper's Ferry armory, West Virginia, former Governor Mosely dispatched messengers to all landowners within a day's ride of Palatka, to a gathering at his mansion. It was not for one of his customary glittering cotillion balls. This time, the only music likely to play would be a drum-roll call to arms.

It was just for landowners. Women were not invited.

That did not sit well with Rebecca Bryant, matriarch of Welaka's leading family.

"I *will* go, and that's that,"she insisted when the messenger attempted to withhold the Governor's note. She read the message addressed to her husband. He was absent again, in Cuba tending to the newspaper he published there, and doing a little merchandising with sugar-cane producers.

'*Juanita*', the steam launch used to ferry merchandise and people between the Bryant warehouse, Palatka and to remote locations along the Ocklawaha River inland toward Ocala, would convey Mrs. Bryant, her 14-year old daughter Octavia – known as 'Tivie' within the family following her little brother Henry's early attempts to pronounce her name – and their neighbor Col. Winston Stephens together with his brother as escort.

There was not much Mrs. Bryant, daughter of the influential mercantile Hall family of Boston and Jacksonville, missed. For many months of the year she ruled the roost where the Byrant family was concerned, and presided over much of the community her erstwhile but erratic husband had founded. For all her staid appearance, emulating the most powerful and admired women in the Victorian-era world, she could tell at a glance by the posture of a porter, whether a package was shy a pound or more, before it was placed on weighing scales.

She wrote a note to Winston and dispatched it with Seth, her cook's boy.

"You be sure to place this in the Colonel's hand, personal. And you wait for his reply. Don't you go wandering off moo-eying Burrel's girls, y'hear?" Her stern warning to Seth, and the exchange of glances between mistress and cook, had him agitated. But it lifted the corners of the cook's lips which turned into a broad, toothy grin, from the messenger's mammy.

The lanky stripling took off, bare foot like all of his kind, loping with easy strides along the wagon-rutted road north, splashing through the shallow ford of Welaka Spring northward to the Colonel's enclave on the bank of the narrow Acosta Creek.

His arrival caused a stir and ripple of excitement to the bucolic routine of the day, especially to one of Burrel's daughters who pretended not to notice.

Winston accepted the note with some trepidation, dismissed Seth with a caution to stay close for a reply, then retired to a shaded porch with a mug of beer and a pipe of home-grown tobacco to read in privacy.

> *Colonel, I would appreciate your company on our journey aboard Juanita to the Governor's meeting on the 29th inst. It will be more comfortable and shorter than the overland route, for you. It will be more comforting and secure for my daughter and I. We would welcome your speedy response. Cordially yours,*
> *Mrs. James Bryant.*

A smoke-filled cough exploded from Winston's face. He had not realized he had been holding his breath all the while until he finished reading, in anticipation of something more dire.

There were unspoken tensions between the Stephens and Bryants ever since he had formally requested Octavia's hand in marriage, two months earlier.

"Absolutely not!" James Bryant responded.

Winston, who had faced brown bears, wild hogs and hostile Indians in the backwoods of Florida, flinched at the virulent response. It shocked him.

Since his return from service, the high regard his company was held in, the success of his plantation and the many pleasant soirees, dances and musical evenings shared within the community, he had assured himself he would win over Octavia's parents as he had captured her affections.

The two men faced each other on either end of the imported Persian rug anchored by the legs of blue silk-embroidered stuffed chairs, in the office-study within the Bryant home at *White Cottage,* in Welaka.

Rebecca had warned her husband something deeper than neighborly affection was brewing between their only daughter and the dashing dark-haired bearded territorial soldier.

"Don't be ridiculous, woman," Bryant, his eyes pouring over documents of laden comparing them to bills and receipts, barely lifted his face from his desk. "She's barely got her breath back from blowing out the birthday candles. Fourteen, as I recall."

"Husband, that is the marrying age in these parts," Rebecca reminded him.

The shuffle of papers paused. He turned a face, deeply lined from four decades of strain through feast and famine as projects succeeded or failed, while siring a handful of his own children. As a man who spent much of his time traveling at home and abroad, he was well aware of casual encounters. His shoulders slumped.

Rebecca seized the opportunity.

"We cannot afford bad blood between neighbors in this community, James. There's enough of that brewing already," her little dig at the tensions between slavers and abolitionists, did not go unnoticed by her Bostonian partner. "Perhaps we should take this opportunity to expand her education in a more civilized society," Rebecca urged. "We could surely find her a good position at the 'Hall Academy for Young Ladies'," she proposed, her cousin's private school in Charleston, South Carolina.

James nodded, but added, "Perhaps she would find more benefit from a wider curriculum and exposure to a more broad metropolitan atmosphere, a little further afield. I have in mind the Richard Parker School for Girls in Boston." He proposed *his* relative.

One thing they both agreed upon. Their daughter ought to marry someone of her station; a professional man with banking, mercantile or legal background. Not a soldier with slaves, corn and cattle to raise.

The stricken look on Winston's face tore into the stern father's resolve. His skills at negotiating deals with fellow merchants, those who had their hands held out and the politicians behind them, were useful in heading off his familial crisis.

"I remember the impatience of youth," he said as he relaxed his stern visage into a smile.

Winston, attuned to any nuance, visibly relaxed, uncurling the fists his hands had bunched into and loosening tensed shoulders.

"Time has a way of sorting things out. Now, I'm not saying yes, or no, for the future. But now is not the right time. It just so happens Octavia will soon be leaving to visit relatives, and broaden her education, with relatives of mine in Boston." The words tumbled out in a torrent to the glee and disappointment of the young soldier.

He had not reached the objective during his first skirmish. But the battle was not yet lost.

~~~

The shiny white pate of the former Governor was a beacon in the crowded reception hall filled with gentlemen planters, yeoman farmers and one women coyly but determinedly, working the room. The former lawyer and legislator, did his best to keep Rebecca Bryant at bay but, as a southern gentleman raised and educated at Chapel Hill, North Carolina, could not ignore her completely.

"My dear Mrs. Bryant. It is such a pleasure to welcome you, once again, to my humble abode."

The rich drapes and plush carpets, brocaded furnishings and family portraits reaching back beyond his 17th Century Virginia ancestors lining the patterned-silk walls, belied his deprecatory status.

"Is it possible there was some misunderstanding regarding the purpose of this gathering?" he posed.

The bushy white eyebrows raised high on his sun-bronzed face toward the distinctive demarcation line created by the rim of his sun-hat. He was not one to loll about his mansion, but was up early to observer his overseers properly dispersed more than a hundred slaves to cotton fields and orange groves, timber felling and fishing tasks. He was wont to appear unannounced and unexpectedly anywhere on his lands, husbanding his property.

"Why the pleasure is surely all mine, Governor," Rebecca smiled tightly. "As you know, in the absence of my dear husband, caring for our holdings in Cuba, he has placed the care and comfort of our community in my frail hands." A firm flick of her black-lace and ebony-spine fan belied her diminutive role. "My husband and I do our best, but do not always see eye to eye, you understand."

Moseley, well aware of the Yankee sympathies and mix of Whig and Democrat harbored on his eastern flank, accepted the undeclared support for his pro-slavery stance. It was no secret, based on his supportive role as Governor to the state of Texas during the recent Mexican-American War. He, like many fellow southerners, considered that conflict a potential expansion of slave-holding territory.

The little cameo of conflict caught the attention of a few gentlemen who empathized with Moseley's predicament from personal experience garnered in surviving in the pioneer state.

Few wandered afield from the source of power to observe a more passionate exchange on the tall-columned portico built to catch prevailing summer breezes from the south-east.

Octavia and Winston were not reaching an understanding.

Mrs. Marion, their chaperon, rocked within earshot with practiced ease on the oak-planked verandah, ostensibly knitting and humming 'Onward Christian Soldiers' in keeping with the theme of the gathering.

"But my dearest darling girl. Surely you see we could be

in great turmoil shortly. You will have need of a protector, to say the very least."

"I have a father, brothers and am not without knowledge and skill, as you are aware, sir." Octavia, for all she was still a child, was an astute observer of how the grown-ups in polite society handled a contretemps.

She also knew, from her days running her hoop through the compact few blocks of waterfront downtown of Jacksonville, how the rougher elements of the community, including sailors and tavern-girls, conducted their affairs. Beneath the puffed fabrics and bustled dresses which effectively swept many a ballroom floor, was a girl capable of holding her own against a household of brothers.

Winston, left fatherless and under his widowed mother's firm hand, had little experience combating female whims and wiles.

He swirled away from her, biting back a sharp rejoinder which, once released, would forever prove fodder in the future. That much he had learned. If there was a future for them to share.

"Pappa was quite clear," Octavia scolded with all the assurance of a young miss in the right. "We are to stay apart until I have reached my majority. Because of you," a flash of anger entered her tone, "I have been exiled to the frozen Yankeeland, forever."

The ever-ready slip of bunched lace handkerchief appeared in her gloved hand to be pressed into moist eyes.

Winston stepped forward to comfort her.

A dry cough reminded him of the protocols.

"There, there, dear. Come and sit by me, for the moment." Mrs. Marion's voice croaked. "I do believe the Governor's meeting is beginning, Colonel."

A beaten-brass gong, normally used to summon family and guests to dine, sounded. Its tone echoed through the house to penetrate lively conversations, raised voices and hearty laughter from the assembled invitees arguing, boasting and bragging in the robust manner of a gathering of men, anywhere.

"Damn!"

The curse escaped Winston's lips, to his chagrin. Octavia had extracted a pledge from him not to curse or blaspheme when in her company, as he did on his plantation.

His error prompted a further cuss. His life was ruined. He stiffly bowed, spun about and swiftly marched into the mansion, muttering barely audible words which caused the Governor's sharp-eared black major-domo, dispatched to round-up attendees, to blanch.

Mrs. Marion tut-tutted while Octavia giggled mischievously.

It was a night to remember.

Chapter 3

Winston Waylaid

Palatka's sparsely-populated community only existed due to the narrowing of the St. Johns River at a wide promontory of the eastern shore at Federal Point which jutted westward, 50-miles south of Jacksonville on the north-flowing river, and shoaled.

It was at the cross-point of a river route north and south with the most direct overland route between the Atlantic harbor of St. Augustine and the new State Capitol of Tallahassee at the midway site selected between east Florida and the Gulf of Mexico port at Pensacola, on its western border with Alabama.

The cow-crossing location had entered its first expansion and development toward a city, following the ousting of its Indian population, and promise of homestead land for war veterans, and cheap arable acres for pioneers.

Steam engines, from boats to trains, grist and saw-mills were beginning to open up the tangled territory. Supplemented by slave labor and transportation options, speculators from mostly southern states flocked into Florida. An army of middlemen marched in lock-step a few paces behind. Merchants selling hardware from chamber pots to hair-ribbons, plus the services of stables and farriers, barbers and bars sprung up along the St. Johns shores wherever steamers could stop and populations settle.

Winston's mind was elsewhere while Governor Moseley and a few other prime movers in the affairs of Putnam County such as secessionist 'Doc' May and his partners, the county's second largest slave-owners. The talk buzzing around his ears was all about protecting property, from buildings to slaves, in the event there should be open conflict beyond conversation, separating northern states from the south.

"What say you, Colonel?"

The courtroom baritone of 'Doc' May, the multi-faceted entrepreneur, penetrated the seething turmoil churning within Winston's head. He had waited so long, fought in the wilderness, faced death and risked all scraping a living from the rich soil on the river banks, to be rejected by a slip of a girl and her Yankee father.

"What?" He snapped a cross response.

"Did we wake you?"

"Not at all."

The soldier summed up the situation swiftly. He could not ignore the titter of amusement of his peers, and the glance of disapproval from his neighbor, Rebecca. While his mind had been occupied with his own travails, his ears heard and automatically processed sense of the talk around him. He caught the gist: barricades, stores, arms, ammunition, communication, raiders, then his name being called.

"Governor, Ma'am, Doctor, gentlemen, we can hold off an attack long enough to escape to safety, inland. But we cannot prevent damage and pillaging if, and when, an armed force gets a foothold. The river will be the front-line, if conflict comes to the county." Winston summed up his assessment.

"Rubbish. We're worth ten of them Yankees," a slurry voice called out.

Applause, foot-stamping mingled with cheers and laughter within the walls of Mosely's mansion.

Winston glowered, but held his own counsel. He caught the eye of the governor peering over the top of wire-rimmed half-glasses and a slight shake of the head.

"Perhaps," the governor's thin piercing voice repeated several times before the audience quieted. "Perhaps the

Colonel can best address that assessment, as a combat veteran..."

The less exuberant shushed others, their eyes focused on the wiry, bearded and browned young man getting to his feet, in their midst. Winston addressed Mosely, but all within the room and, unknown to him, a few near the open windows facing the veranda, listened to a voice honed to be heard above volleys being fired.

"The British, the French and the Indians might disagree with that assessment, sir. Many of our grandparents fought in those same wars, side by side. We know their capabilities, as do they know ours. But, they outnumber us, outspend us, and out-produce us in weapons of war on land and sea. In a war of attrition, it would take a miracle to survive and overcome the Yankees. And do not forget. Not all who occupy the south, are southerners." Winston's eyes swept the room, lingering briefly on Rebecca before returning to Moseley's nodding head.

"I will fight to hold my land, and yours if needs be. But, it's no cake-walk." He shrugged and smiled.

The tension is the room dissipated in the laughter which followed his comment. All faced potential ruin and literal devastation if a rampaging fighting force roamed the land. But, the cheerful image of Sunday afternoons replaced that dismal image. They could all relate to those gatherings of family and friends with a fiddle-player and maybe a piano, strumming out a lively tune. Guests would demurely dance first, then perhaps conclude with an exhilarating polka. While they sat to recover, some glad-rag-clad slaves took the floor. Guests fanned themselves and sipped punch and closely observed the entertainment of competing darkies who hurled themselves into uninhibited jigs, combining hip-wriggling and stomping in a wild rhythmic manner.

Naturally, with a competition came a little side-bet to enliven the event, plus suitable cheers of encouragement and many raised glasses, until a winner was chosen to take the cake, prepared by the host's mammy.

That lifestyle could die, too, if troops ran amok. Or, encouraged the slaves to revolt and run away.

"Well said, sir," Mosely praised Winston's response. "It is our intent to form a front-line volunteer defense and mounted guerrilla force until such time as this business is settled in Washington." A chorus of boos and hisses near drowned him out. "Until such time we seek our southern separatist sovereignty…"

Those words triggered applause and wild yelps likened to a pack of wolves howling at a full-moon. It was a sound which echoed through bayous and off river-banks, through wooded hollows and across marshland and prairie for years to come. A cry which became familiar to a nation, embroiled in a civil war, as the Rebel Yell.

When the exuberance subsided and the clinking of glasses diminished while planters resumed their seats, the somber dark figure of Rebecca Bryant rose to her feet.

"Mister Governor, mister governor," the lilt of her southern tongue swept through those assembled at the mansion with the enveloping flow of syrup or molasses over pancakes. "I applaud your efforts to provide a picket fence to keep the hordes at bay; if it should come to that."

There was some muted mumbling of support from the gentlemen surrounding her, who had modified their language in deference to her presence. Others, who had dealt with James Bryant's wife before, held back, waiting for the second shoe to fall.

"However. . ."

"Here it comes," whispered one observer.

"…on day two, and day fifty-two, and one-hundred-and-two of the perilous time ahead we had best be prepared and dug in away from our homes, farms and all we hold dear for, mark my words, it will be a battle of attrition and policy of scorched-earth we face." Her finger wagged high above her head similar to a Sunday preacher delivering a sermon. "Prepare your weapons, but store your supplies."

Her words were lost in the conflicting responses, un-regulated this time, vented by confident armchair warriors. Winston stepped forward to escort her from the room. She chuckled behind her fan.

"You think that maybe stirred them up?" she asked. "When they look back on this night in the cold of dawn, beyond their thick heads and furry tongues, a few will remember my words. Their course will not change, but their tactics for survival, might save the lives of their families, and slaves."

Winston found himself nodding in agreement. His thoughts had been focused on recruitment, available riders, horses, weapons while the plantation – his livelihood – slipped into the background. Resistance without resilience would not win the day.

The seeds of secession were planted and took root in the minds of many who had ignored the issue, until that night.

~~~

The double-blast of the side-wheeler's steam-horn alerted any other river-craft to beware when lines were cast off the long dock extending into Palatka Bay, allowing the *Hattie Belle* to depart, taking Tivie and her mother away from Winston.

He stood still and stoic amongst the surrounding crowd waving departure to the excited passengers, craning against the rails for a final glimpse, before the churning paddles powered forward and back to spine the river-boat's bow north for her journey to Jacksonville.

The sudden change of plan, to return to Welaka aboard *Juanita,* was not revealed until they clambered into the carriage which would return them to the dock.

"I'm afraid this is where we must say our goodbyes, for the present," Rebecca leaned forward to place a lace-gloved hand on Winston's knee. His eyes swung from Tivie who pointedly paid great attention to passing pedestrians clumping along raised wooden sidewalks.

"What do you mean?"

"As my dear husband explained, our daughter needs to pursue a further education and prepare for her coming-out where she will be presented to society." Mrs. Bryant pressed on, gripping Winston's thigh almost to the point of pain.

He winced at the news and the touch.

"Once she has completed her formal obligatory tasks and returns to our home, here, her future will be decided." She squeezed again.

"Ouch. That smarts," he complained, to the amusement of Tivie.

She giggled, knowing well the controlling tricks of her mother who raised four irascible boys. For the moment his immediate concern was to wriggle free, without the fuss of fanning a feud into open hostility.

Then the full-impact of what was about to happen, sunk in on Winston. Under the pretext of attending the governor's meeting, he had happily provided protection and aided in the escape of his intended bride with no protest or fireworks.

Colonel Stephens had been out-maneuvered by a diminutive but skillful opponent, with not a shot fired.

A blood-moon, large and orange, rose from the silhouette of the pine and live-oak forested bank along the eastern shore. Drooping layers of sphagnum-moss draped from spindly misshapen branches like locks of hair from a witches head. It contained beauty and macabre images to adult and child alike. The woods surrounding those few patches of Florida's inhabited land, held hope and horror of both known and unknown perils still to be discovered.

An involuntary chill briefly shook Winston watching the fading lights and subsiding wake of the steamer fade into the distance. The crowd around him dispersed until he felt a tug on his jacket.

"Winnie," his brother Swep called. "Let's go. The night is still young and the tables are calling."

Within the emerging community of Palatka, along with

the few hostelries and boarding houses dotting its laid-out streets spreading out like wagon-wheel spokes from the square-grid of the community center, informal drinking houses of entertainment had arrived.

"No. I'm not in..." he began.

"This will get you started," a hip-flask was thrust into his hand by a friend of his brother, a brawny youth, sometime fisherman, sometime farmer. A bunch of like-thinking bachelors, drawn to the Stephens brothers who had a reputation up and down the river of high-jinks and good men in a brawl, began to chant.

"Drink it down, drink it down, she's out of town, she's out of town."

There were few secrets in a small community.

"Hell with it," Winston cussed.

He took a long swallow of the fiery home-brewed liquor which triggered dormant beer and champagne already in his system. It was the first of many that night, those who remember any details recall. None would ever reveal the name of the woman Winston woke up in bed with the next morning.

Palatka was abuzz with reports and speculations based on stories emerging about the meeting at the mansion. There was an urgency in the air which mounted during the following months and years of Democrat James Buchanan's waffling presidency, until anti-secessionist Republican Abraham Lincoln won election to the Presidency.

The turmoil which followed barely registered in the mind and heart of Winston when he realized he had lost his true love and sinned with a substitute which tormented his every waking hour.

PART III

Midshipman in Navy Blue

Chapter 1

Midshipman in Navy Blue

New Jersey fog enveloped its coast far out to sea where, even on a clear day, the Atlantic sea was shallow enough to drop anchor out of sight of land.

"By the mark 10."

The call of the boy seaman trembled the first time he dropped the lead-line over the side, blindfolded. The hand of a leading seaman fingered the material; a piece of leather with a hole in it, nodded his head to the Midshipman aboard the navy department's Coast Survey schooner *Jersey II*, hove-to awaiting the sun's rays to burn away the night fog.

"Very good Jenkins. Now let's see what's under our arse, eh?"

The unexpected joke from an officer brought a chuckle from the leads man and his trainees. But Midshipman Samuel Taylor was not like any of the other officers aboard, by a long shot. That was one area of agreement upper and lower deck conceded

The onetime stowaway boy with his cat, who had crept aboard the yacht *America* a decade earlier, had bulked up during the intervening years.

'Sammy', Samuel or Sam, as his closest friends within the navy and the pilots who competed for business for all vessels venturing into New York's tricky harbor called him, had shot up in stature by a full six inches during his between years. Now, on the eve of his 21st birthday which would also celebrate his status as a 'passed' Midshipman, he was a hair shy of six-feet tall.

"Captain on deck." A cry from the quartermaster alerted all to the presence of Lt. Valentine emerging from his cabin.

"Perhaps we'll check the head, eh?" Sam spun on his heel and led his little training team away. Two other boys and an ordinary seaman traipsed behind him while he deftly avoided freshly-scrubbed sections of deck in the waist of the schooner, buckets of soapy waters and jets of brine sprayed from hoses fed from pumps manned by the morning watch.

"Taylor. A word if it pleases you. But, perhaps you already know?"

The piping voice laced with sarcasm sliced through the gray air, raising heads of the bare-foot scrubbing seamen. Sam sighed. He had not been quite quick enough to escape the skipper's notice.

"Carry on, Martin." Sam handed over the stick of chalk and small slate-tablet used to teach lessons on, which he had pressed into service to keep score of his trainees, returned the seaman's salute and retraced his steps to whatever fate awaited him on the quarterdeck. Hopefully not another mishap on the captain's swinging-bed cover, created by one of the late Bambino's off-spring, the black-coated, blue-eyed Sambuca.

"Ah, Mister Taylor, how good of you to spare me the time."

There was no love between Valentine, the languid senior officer and the younger man whose journey aft the mast, through the hawser, was based on his piloting ability. He also had the powerful patronage of one of the naval family of Porters. While Valentine was the figurehead officer aboard, the power behind his vessel's movement lay within the machinations of Coast Survey office. It was one such power player, David Dixon Porter, former surveyor and protégée of the aged founder of the department, Swiss mathematician Ferdinand Hassler, who had hoisted the newly passed midshipman out of obscurity to help chart the coast.

"Have you breakfasted?"

"No sir."

"Oh, that's too bad. Perhaps the bum-boat will have something aboard. But your trip ashore should not take more than, a few hours, eh?" Valentine smiled tightly in the growing light which signaled the dispersal of fog-banks rolling along the coast between Sandy Hook and the shoals of Delaware Bay.

It marked the conclusion of the latest contretemps to occur between the two.

~~~

Their plodding progress inched across the seabed, charting safe-passage for future mariners, aboard the shallow draft Dutch-built craft with hefty lee-boards to prevent drift. The lazy ocean rollers lifted the craft a good six feet higher to view the unbroken horizon, clear except for the activity of a flock of seagulls ahead. It was directly in their path.

Sam clambered into the shrouds, telescope secured until he had a clear view ahead.

"Object in the water, dead ahead." He called a warning down.

"Just bait fish, Mister Taylor," replied the ship's sailing master.

"No sir. I beg to differ. There's something solid beneath them." There was an edge of urgency in Sam's voice.

"What's going on here?" Valentine's thin call preceded him up the steps from his cabin.

"It's a wreck!"

The certainty in Sam's voice caught the attention of all on deck. The boatswain and senior hands moved toward their stations in anticipation of orders.

"Nonsense. It's a sandy bottom for a thousand hectares. We've plumbed damned near every one, so far." Valentine's tight smile caught the Master's eye. But that man's expression was worried. "Surely you don't think..."

"Wreck ahead, off the starboard bow," cried a lookout.

"Hard about!" the master urgently called to the helmsman. He assisted to thrust the tiller across the width of the quarterdeck, chasing Lt.Valentine from his up-wind perch.

Jersey II tilted abruptly from her level course across the silent rollers to steeply plunge her nose and rise again. The rudder dug in, the lee-board dropped below the surface, sails and rigging flapped and rattled overhead and her bow swung about.

"Heave to," the officer of the deck piped up when she resumed her new course.

They sat rolling on the sea, all straining to see what the ship's launch would discover when it reached the patch of swirling water being dove upon by a variety of seabirds from pip-squeak black-headed sandpipers to yellow-beaked wide-winged seagulls.

Down below, the sounds of spilled wooden bowls, pewter plates and mugs being gathered from the lower-deck where they had slid to from the mess-tables, was a reminder of the damage caused in the emergency maneuver. The cost might be laid at Midshipman Taylor's door, according to the captain, if it turned out to be a false alarm.

The culprit was confined to the upper-deck, much to the amusement of his fellow officers, enjoying the break from their monotonous tasks. Jenkins, the captain's steward, scowled when he emerged on deck bearing a basket of cracked and shattered pottery what had been staked for washing before his small pantry unexpectedly tipped and tumbled everything to an unforgiving deck. The plop-plop-plop of plates hitting water seemed to echo the nails Sam felt were being hammered into his career coffin.

"They're coming back."A call from the masthead merely confirmed what all could see. Bent backs swayed in rhythm to the rise and fall of oars, the coxswain stoically steered toward the ship and the captain's eyes swept across the sea capturing no one's gaze aboard.

"Reckon you got away with it," the hoarse whisper of the doughty old master drifted over to Sam's ear. A murmured low-key cheer rose from the men leaning over the side, watching every nuance aboard the approaching boat; including a furtive thumbs-up from the bowman who arose with his boat-hook at the ready.

Sam expelled a long-held breath, and rapped his knuckles on the varnished binnacle-casing enclosing the brass-framed compass. His abilities to read the sea, noted long ago by pilot captain Brown, had not betrayed him.

"What was it?" the master asked. "Could have been a whale."

"The pattern of the water flow across the tide and sea surge," Sam muttered. "It indicated something solid, and big, was sitting just below the surface."

The master smiled. "Best call it second-sight, eh? Keep 'em guessin'." He winked.

Sam's sharp eye for registering what he observed and considering the possibilities had made the difference between he and competitors who only saw what they expected. It proved helpful in the ever-shifting sand-bars subject to tide and storm, guarding the entrance to New York City.

A few years earlier, when rumblings of internecine warfare reached boiling point, Sam's sea sense and piloting ability caused a change in career course.

Captain David Dixon Porter, an unusually talented naval officer with a multi-faceted mix of service and family ties, had heard of young Samuel Taylor's prowess. Porter's own nautical career had zigged and zagged between the United States naval and merchant marine, depending on war or peace periods.

At one time Jefferson Davis, the then American Secretary of War, commissioned Porter to take the store-ship USS *Supply* to the middle-east to round up camels as transportation beasts of burden to deploy in desert-like western states. Ripples from that failed venture long outlived both men. The vigilant, multi-faceted sailor had also once been assigned as a member of the office of Coastal Survey during the reign of Swiss political refugee, the late Professor Hasslar, its first Superintendent.

By chance Porter dined at the New York Yacht Club with Commodore John Cox Stevens and heard about his protégé's role in *America*'s race, and subsequent position as a harbor pilot. Porter, despite the fug of brandy and cigar-smoke, had a suggestion.

"I think, Commodore, this young man might best serve his country as a navigator and surveyor, rather than routine tasks in and out of the harbor. We both know war is inevitable. Control of the coast, shipping and ports, will be vital."

The Commodore's patriotic and paternal interests melded. Within days he and Brown plotted a professional course for their protégé. The stowaway-waif's life took another unexpected turn when he found himself volunteered into the US Navy by his patrons.

~~~

His life was about to take another spin, that day off-shore of the New Jersey coast.

Puzzled, Sam took the folded parchment thrust into his hand by Lt. Valentine, to swiftly scan and solve the mystery which so amused his captain.

He felt a flash of anger, joy and a sense of relief at its contents.

Dated October 26, 1861, it bore orders to forthwith proceed to the New York Navy Yard where he would help prepare the steam gunboat *Ottawa* for sea-trials, assume the duties of navigation officer at the newly commissioned rank of Lieutenant. His joy was marred by the Valentine's spite which had withheld the news.

He had certainly received it the moment the supply cutter had bumped alongside in pre-dawn darkness. Sam felt small comfort that the dispatches contained within the water-proofed weighted message-bag had to have awoken Valentine the moment it arrived.

"And you can take that blasted cat with you, too." Valentine nodded curtly and scuttled back to his quarters without a further word.

His comment barely penetrated the swirl of emotions Sam experienced. Automatically he acknowledged the handshakes and comments from crew, civilian surveyors and brother officers stationed aboard who instantly picked up the scuttlebutt. In a scurry of activity his kit was packed by the steward's black assistant, his dress-uniform was exchanged for his workaday outfit, leather shore-shoes replaced the canvas and rope-soled sea-shoes, and a thick-sliced fresh-baked bacon and egg sandwich found its way into his hands.

"Where's Sambuca?"he cried out when the small crowd of well-wishers urged him toward the anxiously-waiting cutter alongside, its sails flapping lazily in the light wind awaiting the order to haul in the sheets, tighten up and cast off.

"Here he is sir, here he is."

The ship's sail-maker handed over a writhing small kitbag punctured with brass grommets too small for a paw to find purchase, but wide enough to allow air – and perhaps some bow-spray - aboard the lolling cutter on its trip ashore.

"Hush now, hush." Sam tucked the bag and its confined creature under his arm while somehow managing hand-shakes, farewells and a precarious descent from *Jersey*'s rounded hull onto the bouncing gunwale of the boat below.

Several hands reached to prevent his tumble and within moments they were cast-off and heading toward the next chapter in an eventful decade.

Chapter 2

Homesick

Octavia's big adventure in Boston unraveled with the reality of the northern state's marrow-freezing cold. No matter how many layers of chamois she wore under her fashionable dresses echoing the latest ladies styles portrayed in the pages of Harper's Magazine, she felt frozen.

Even her tiny white teeth chattered so much she seemed afflicted with stuttering.

"Oh Amy, how can you stand it?" she asked her closest friend, an auburn-haired, pale-skinned wraith who seemed to float effortlessly across the patterned marbled floors of the lyceum for young ladies that they attended.

Tivie's visions of candle-lit ballrooms glittering with the reflected light from crystal-draped chandeliers, with mulled-wine, roaring fires and eager, smartly uniformed young gentlemen crowding around her awaiting their name to show on her dance-card, had not anticipated the academic side of the equation.

Amy, who had spent her first dozen years living in Fort Sandusky on the south shore of Lake Erie, where her father traded animal pelts for hardware and cash to trappers and Indian scouts, shrugged.

"Honey," she echoed Tivie's favorite form of address. "Wait til winter gets here."

She withdrew a slender hand from the mink-muff she affected when not writing to her many beaus, acquired like trinkets at a gift-shop from the fort, to sweep in the newly-opened Christmas presents still displayed around the room.

Tivie pulled the somber tasseled shawl about her and suddenly laughed.

"What?"

"Oh Amy, dear, I'm sure I must look just like a real Granny McGree."

They both laughed at the image of the nickname they had bestowed on all the black-cloth clad ancient Irish worshipers who daily passed the scrubbed doorsteps of the Richard Parker School for Girls, back and forth to services at Franklin Street Cathedral.

"Oh yes, Mrs. McGree. And how is yer darlin' soldier-boy today?" Amy teased in a mock accent.

There were few secrets withheld between the two who, though poles apart in outlook and upbringing, had quickly taken to each other in their isolation.

Tivie extracted the latest *billet doux* from her Southern gentleman admirer, as she referred to Winston in far off, warm, Florida, from the ever-present muff. Its presence in her hands while listening to the little talks concerning everything from the appropriate china pattern correct for the occasion, to thread-count in cotton-sheets for children to counts, linked her to home.

"It is a worry," she confessed, unfolding the letter to reveal his precise, forward-sloping words horizontal this time. Sometimes, when he had a lot of information; usually about the plantation, crops, family and neighborhood events, the writing ran horizontal and vertical on all concealed surfaces except the last fold which bore her name and address.

She quoted:

'Dear Tivie,

The hours, days, weeks without you are empty of your sunshine which lights up my life and warms my heart, as I wish I could warm yours in that freezing Yankee town, as you say. I cross notch the days to your return, under our names, on that tree in our grove.'

She glanced up at Amy.

"We discovered a darling glade to picnic one spring when new grass shoots and leaves burst bright and green from ground, bush and tree. Spotted fawns wobbled about on spindly legs, weaning from their mothers to the fresh provender supplied in God's garden. A perfect setting, with colorful scarlet and yellow black-eyed Susans raising their heads toward the sun beams filtering through the branches."She sighed, then shivered from the reality of their frigid room.

'I have sited Rose Cottage close to the path from Welaka, kitty-cornered so we can see visitors approaching from a way off to prepare for their arrival.'

Tivie inclined her free hand at an angle to indicate the position of the house, then tossed a cupped-hand toward her lips mimicking the movements of a drinker.

Amy giggled.

"We had talked of having our home on the banks of the St. Johns so we could get the full view of the glorious sunsets," Tivie sighed. "The one from the heavens and the other reflected on the river surface. But the colonel reckons all the agitation for separation will in all likelihood, come to armed conflict between states, and neighbors. Why, even in my family there are divisions. Pappa is a Yankee at heart and opposes our independence, even though he and his kin fought for their own freedom, from the British." Her foot stamped on the colorful rag-rug under the desk, muffling the sound of heels on her eye-and-hook boot.

Amy's expression did not change, but within, turmoil raged. A child of the frontier army, she was isolated in a city which saw itself as the champion of civility, sophistication and equality, providing of course, those less equal kept their place. The great port, the international bustle of imports and exports, played host to citizens of every known civilization who were as likely to be roaming its streets, supping at its coffee-shops, scouring the shelves of its bookshops, as a drover bringing sheep to the slaughter-house.

Her diminutive friend from the south, for all her dainty poise and molasses manners was no soft blossom which could be crushed in a strong grip. More like a succulent flowering cactus; pleasing to the eye but deadly if mishandled. In the privacy of their room, along with all the girl-talk, tales of trapping, fishing and hunting with her brothers and that Indian-fighter colonel of hers bore echoes of Amy's own tomboy leanings.

In a fort full of soldiers, some not old enough to shave, and others a whisker away from the whipping-post, she learned how to fend for herself. Reason enough, according to her mother, to dispatch her to boarding-school and prepare her for a life of domesticity.

'*Dear Tivie,*' the Southern belle continued, '*I know in my heart we should be married now. And except for such restrictions and promises extracted from us, we would be as one, now. Your folks, dear as they are to me as upright neighbors and a sanctuary of civilization in the wonderful wilderness we are taming, are locked into old traditions. One day, perhaps too late for us, they will come to realize a marriage forged through the heat of love is stronger than one arranged for financial or political gain.*"

Both young ladies and their contemporaries at the academy shared different viewpoints regarding the selection of their intended life-partners. After all, they would not be attending a finishing school if it were not to learn how to follow the social mores and protocols of the era, Amy had pointed out when her friend ate her first dinner.

"Like this," she whispered to the new girl seated next to her in the dining hall. Deftly she speared a morsel of meat, a smidgen of potato and a few peas onto the down-turned tines of the silver fork, pressed it firmly with the knife-blade, and demurely engulfed it behind pouty-lips firmly-closed while the mouthful was masticated the appropriate 25-times before being swallowed.

Octavia Bryant, smartly dressed in last-year's style, glanced at the other plates placed on the fine linen tablecloth where other young ladies watched with hawk-eyes, every move she made. The rustic habit of impaling food with a fork, cutting it, reversing the fork to scoop the individual items up to transfer, was frowned upon.

"It's not what the Queen would do, is it?"

That comment covered every action throughout the day into nighttime preparations, by teachers and senior girls appointed as prefects to aide – or spy and tittle-tattle as the juniors considered it – while the finer points of social etiquette were enforced.

"Why do they defer to the Queen of England, so? This is the heart of rebellion, where the tea-party was held in protest against Britain."

Octavia's first days at the academy had been filled with questions. Amy's know-how through the close-knit military families who did everything by the book, rules and regulations, knew many of the answers.

"It's part of the pecking-order. There are those, still, who would exchange a portion of their wealth for a knighthood title or listing amongst the peerage. They not only want power from wealth, but the prestige of lording it over everyone with a title."

Amy, a child within an extended family which knew its place from foot-soldier to Brigadier-General, was scornful of speculators who wielded so much influence.

Chapter 3

Anaconda

Tensions between political parties in the backrooms of the District of Columbia, and those attending social events in the brick and marble residences lining Washington's streets criss-crossing Capitol Hill, had hostesses on edge.

In addition to concerns whether the right invited people would appear, that there were no disasters in the kitchen and additional hired staff did not get into the liquor, an outbreak of dueling was sweeping the city.

Sophia, wife of the British Minister appointed as ambassador during President Patrick Buchanan's tenure and now attending the lanky Abraham Lincoln's administration, was most upset. A body had been found in the 'Garden of Repose', at the foot of their property.

"I'm sure they had no intent to specifically spoil your event, m'dear. It will all be taken care of and no one any the wiser, before the first guest alights from his carriage," Richard Bickerton Pemel Lyons tried to placate his wife.

"Oh Bicky. It's so upsetting. And now, with all this talk of war, people have started to hoard. You know, we had an awful time securing quail eggs. We'll have to make do with caviar." She pursed her lips.

"It could be due to the season," her husband smiled above the fringe of beard which outlined his jaw. "Perhaps you will have better luck, in the spring."

Sophia's eyes widened, she shook her head and floated away with a handful of notes and her ever-ready cedar-wood graphite pencil poised for action.

The ambassador smiled but ignored the domestic chaos reigning throughout the house, withdrawing to the sanctity of his book-lined study. He also had notes to study. A little weightier than seating arrangements, floral centerpieces and placement of ice-buckets to ensure chilled wines for the fish-course. Only moments before a sealed package had been slipped into his hand by his butler-cum-bodyguard, Jenkins.

A quick glance at the handwriting confirmed his fears. Only under the most dire circumstances would his source at the White House risk indirect contact. His heart quickened in anticipation. The entire country knew what the threat was, and why. But few knew the when and where.

~~~

Brian Hawkins shifted his stance, flipped a page of his sketch-pad over and sauntered to the port-side of the rumbling steamboat pushing a bow-wave to set small boats bobbing and tied craft straining their lines on either side of the river road from north to south, the Mississippi.

The well-dressed but not dandified gentleman traveled alone, tending his own affairs, locking his deck-cabin door whenever he entered or left. During his time aboard he had met and mingled with the cluster of passengers boarding and departing at regular and impromptu stops along the hundred and fifty miles between Baton Rouge and Vicksburg. Occasionally he would display a water-color he had rendered depicting the wharves and warehouse, cotton-bales and barrels being loaded by barely-clad enough for decency, slaves. The crack of a whip seldom touched the black skin, for fear of damaging the hired dockers Hawkins learned. But shiny old scars on the backs of some of the slaves indicated not all overseers were as accurate as they bragged.

"They do say, the best can take the cheroot right out of your mouth," drawled one learned traveler, puffing on a thin Cuban cigarillo. "Sooner thee than me, though," he coughed, laughing at his own quip.

The artistic passenger amiably responded with a nod of the head, while his eyes darted from shore to pad, capturing the activity ashore. A building close to the harbor-master's office had a cluster of men around a wagon unloading long wooden boxes which bore a close resemblance to crates used to ship Lee Enfield rifles. In his official role as armaments officer at Fort Drake, Iowa, he was fully aware of the distinctive shape of the rope-handled cargo.

Mister smoker casually glanced at the younger man's rendering of the pastoral setting and nodded approval. "Caught that scene better than a Bradley. No blurs there, eh?"

They both laughed at the shortcomings of the newly popularized photographic illustrations appearing in some magazines at home and abroad, beginning to edge into the pages reflecting world events. Posed, and sometimes, pinioned people with their heads firmly clamped facing the camera-lens, were the norm. The flow of action could not be captured as accurately as the swift strokes of a sketcher's pen, yet.

The shadow of an evening cloud darkened the sky for a moment. Lanterns were having their wicks trimmed on the bridge. A cats-paw ripple moved across the river surface and the ship's bell sounded briskly, alerting diners to the meal awaiting them.

"See you at our regular table, then?"

"Yes sir, just put my gear away, wash-up and tidy." His sketch-hand lifted in acknowledgment.

The broken door-lock was obvious the moment he stepped back onto the cabin-deck. Swiftly he entered the small space and knew the moment he saw the bunk-mattress askew that it had been no ordinary theft. Before calling the alarm he closed the door behind him. Quickly he felt under one of the wooden slats supporting the mattress. The package of inked renderings remained.

"Thief, thief !" His panicked voice carried far afield seconds later when he regained the cabin deck. A buzz of excited speculation, and official appearance of the deck-officer on duty, completed the scene as the distraught young man was led away to the saloon-bar for many words of solace, and much tut-tutting by the ladies.

His coughing companion, with a fresh Cuban cigarillo, lurked in the background, eyes narrowed. The Yankee did not appear to be as upset as he should have been at losing a month's worth of gathered intelligence. Maybe a more personal mishap needed to befall the civilian snooper, with the military bearing.

~~~

Ambassador Lyons glanced at notations in the White House message and compared them to the wall-map of North America before him. His finger traced the outline of the Atlantic coast from Norfolk, Virginia, down and around Florida's sparsely populated shoreline to sweep along southern states bordering the Gulf of Mexico to the mouth of the Mississippi. His eyes followed the meandering life-line of commerce which thrust upward into the heartland of the westward expanding country.

Lyons nodded his head in agreement with the Federal tactic conceived by Lincoln's overweight commander in chief's perceptive plan, code-named 'Anaconda' according to the message.

It called for the total blockade of all trade in or out of southern ports from established harbors to inlets and creeks. And, an assault upon the numerous townships developing along the banks of the muddy river; from its delta base of New Orleans in Louisiana to Cairo at its junction with the Ohio River in Illinois. The stranglehold on commerce with the ability to swiftly move troops on controlled waterways – liquid highways – could control the secessionists ambitions.

"Yes, but?" Lyons mused, "does America have the stomach for an extended war?"

Earlier he and the French Minister, at a *tete a tete* following an obligatory attendance for the swearing-in of William H. Seward as the newest U.S. Secretary of State, the potential for mischief within European courts and the emerging power-brokers already calculating profits from conflict, had led to a lively discussion.

"Surely, *mon ami*, the Southern gentlemen will sober up in time to realize they can get what they want with the majority seating they have in the House and Senate. This woodsman President, Lincoln, is powerless. A figurehead."

"I think not, Count. It is, as you say, a numbers game, so far. But once the secessionists withdraw to their sovereign south, and the shine wears off the silver crown, they will realize the engine which drives this growing country lies under the smoke-stacks of its industrial north – not the cotton-fields and chivalry of the south," Lyons responded.

Instinctively they turned to view the cluster of patrician figures clustered around the ever-smiling and graceful leader of the Senate, Jefferson Davis and Varina, his wife. In that light from flickering candles reflected through crystal chandeliers, the gaunt-faced Kentuckian bore a remarkable resemblance to the newly elected, hollow-cheeked, President Lincoln.

The Englishman, a collector of relics in the form of coins found in Europe and Turkey, where he had been aide to his father, the British Minister to the Otterman Court, wondered whose profile would grace the coinage of a post Civil War America.

Chapter 4

First Round

A bed chamber-pot with the image of President Lincoln reproduced inside, was the scandalous talk of the quilting club when the first delivery of porcelain pots appeared in Wallace's hardware store window on Main Street, Palatka.

It was the latest flamboyant demonstration of the South's disregard for the slave-freeing President whose brief tenure in the nation's capitol would be ended soon, within days, weeks, months at the most. So said the ebullient supporters of President Jefferson Davis' newly formed Confederacy.

"If push comes to shove," a cotton-grower confided loudly at a well-provisioned table in a Charleston tavern, "we can handle those Yankee blue-coats in a few weeks, or a month at the most."

Tankards pounded the bar and table by supporters of the popular sentiment. A newly arrived gray-clad reefer, as Midshipman were nicknamed, whispered to his companion and brother.

"Take a large pinch of salt if you want to swallow that one. At the academy, before we went our separate ways, I was twice bested by Yanks in fair fights and foul, you know." He pinched the mature judge affectionately but effectively, on the thigh.

"Gracious!" A muffled squeal and slop of beer, brought an instant response. "You really must learn to control your impulses, Jimmy. We're not in the playground, now."

The cross reply was expected. The younger, smaller brother, the baby of a baker's dozen children brought up in New Orleans, learned early how to use all his wiles; from biting, kicking, scratching, crying and smiling, to survive and get his way. Overcoming his natural exuberance with the need for careful consideration was a difficult lesson to learn emerging from a college atmosphere to the real world. His transition from pupil to serving officer was abrupt.

One day his Annapolis classmates and teachers were focused on nautical matters from trigonometry to the study of heavenly bodies to determine where in the world they were at, the next day they were akimbo, guided by their hearts and homeland to scatter north, and south. Earlier in the year, aboard the training ship *Santee* during a brief courtesy call to the Boston seaport, fisticuffs had come into play to protect a southern belle-in-training.

In the morn he would regain the ship he had been assigned to and help launch the long-awaited assault on the Federal Fort Sumter. He anticipated the first shots of war with dread and eager anticipation. Unlike most of the well-clad clients of the tavern, he had seen the results a 32-pound cannon-ball could create on the most hearty sailor, rending it in twain, both parts flopping and spouting blood until the heart drained and the brain mercifully closed down, dead.

"Try to stay out of trouble, remember to duck and, for our mother's sake, no more gory trophies." The elder brother, in his turn, prodded the young officer's thigh with sufficient force to extract a yelp.

Their exchanged glances reflected a shared memory of the shriveled ears of a pirate, lopped-off as souvenirs during an assault of a Caribbean atoll anchorage.

"Right, sir. Rules of war apply during this conflict. No savage barbarism as displayed by the scum floating on the high seas. At least," he added, "that's the word from on high – so far."

~~~

The bombardment and speedy surrender of the keystone fort and port on the eastern seaboard was a severe strategic blow to Lincoln's strategy and a morale boost to Davis's ill-equipped military forces.

A spectator, and speculator, from the British isles, introduced to society as Lord Henry Edward Darcie shrewdly summed up the alternatives open to his southern host, who held the financial reins in his grasp, thus the power and access to leaders of the newly-formed government.

Titled gentry, even though only from the embittered and torn country of Ireland, was something of a coup amongst Charleston's insular society. And the affable gentleman's arrival in the much admired, newly acquired, racing yacht *America* which had beaten the best Britain could muster, was symbolic and timely. She represented what could be achieved, against great odds. More importantly, from the sparse supply of shipping available to the Confederacy, a potential addition to its arsenal.

The possibilities had not escaped the rather mysterious and somewhat vague background of the sophisticated, knowledgeable and adept captain. His proposed voyage to the far-flung outposts of the British Empire 'Down Under' had taken an abrupt 90-degree turn, upon learning of the former American colony's potential civil conflict, while ashore in the Azores.

Captain Darcie took his host, family and friends including a local judge and his pipsqueak younger brother wearing a gray, brand new tailored Confederate naval uniform on a day-sail. The outing, presided over by his recently acquired wife and half a dozen of her children, appeared to be naught but a pleasant day of relaxation. However, each had their own point of view to pursue.

One such was English cotton merchant Charles Green. He and one of the captains of his shipping line, closely observed the schooner's maneuverability; speed on a variety of courses, steadfastness when she poked her nose into blustery

Atlantic seas. They laughed and cried in alarm, with the ladies and children when a salty spray swept back from the bow. But exchanged significant glances, knowing full well a similar blow would have sent all hands tumbling, and a sheet of solid water flushing the decks. *America* swept across the waves unperturbed, at speed in excess of any of their ships designated as blockade runners.

The young confederate midshipman thrilled at the lively ride aboard what was still considered to be the fastest yacht in the world.

"You're a little out of date, old son," the judge teased. "She lost a couple of races, I heard, in subsequent challenges."

"Facts, dear brother. She was unceremoniously dumped by her Yankee investors to get their dollars back. They dined off her victory for years before even considering offering the cup up in challenge. The boat-builders pined for her, and began filling orders for private owners which filled the banker's coffers broadened the New York Yacht Club's membership base. Those board members recouped their investments again, and allowed the fees to underwrite all costs." The midshipman rattled off his version of events.

"But..."

"No buts, dear brother. She passed from hand to hand, was neglected, damn near rotted away and had an ocean of seaweed and a crowded aquarium attached to her bottom, during those races." Their conversation above the wind and shrieking children, being children, was overheard and repeated by more than one observer.

Darcie, who tuned his responses to queries depending who posed them, appeared oblivious to the undercurrents flowing about him. Observers were misled if they drew that conclusion. He was aware of the cost, and scarcity any sizable vessel which could be pressed into service by the skimpy gray navy. The dangerous role he played could collapse if a belligerent general stepped in to seize his vessel if he pressed for too high a price. Once she was out of sight and shore-bound without compensation, the newly-formed Darcie family would be near destitution, save a title.

After-dinner cigars and drinks that night accompanied light banter and heavy negotiating between the English southern gentleman and his guest, avidly followed by a wide-eyed and newest ' officer and gentleman' created by the Confederate Commander-in-Chief.

A sum of $60,000 would be paid for *America*, but she would remain a British-registered vessel under the command of Darcie, who claimed the rank of Royal Navy Captain during the Napoleonic wars, thus retaining neutrality.

"I would gladly board a steamer, with the memsahib and tribe, for a leisurely cruise around the world while you chaps brawl amongst yourselves." He swirled brandy in the bubble-glass, inhaling its aroma before sipping it. An inch of ash clung to the cigar held steady in his other hand, languidly draped along the brocaded armchair he casually sprawled into.

Green smiled.

He shrewdly weighed the measure of the man and his vessel against the needs of himself and the newly-formed confederacy. The fee, considering the circumstances, was reasonable. Normal northern sources were out of the question. British shipbuilders and owners were holding out for exorbitant amounts and the French were being, French. Time and deadlines stretched to a point where, once the last *sou* was extracted from the buyer's account, excuses were made to deny delivery.

He raised his own snifter to nod agreement.

Unofficially, at that moment, *America* became a southern naval asset.

Part IV

Transition

Chapter 1

Transition

Following the first salvos of secession and the fall of Fort Sumter, there was an apparent lull in aggressive activity. It was a readjustment by both sides who finally faced the reality of physical, rather than verbal, assault.

Not much of a military nature changed, in the rural patch of Putnam County divided by the liquid-highway of the St. Johns River, and the frontier community of Welaka. Craft of all types conveyed supplies overseas from Fernandino at the Georgia border or the city of Jacksonville. Each city was connected by rail to the north which brought manufactured items from nails to build homes and barns and steam-engines to drive saw-mills. In return, raw materials like cotton, indigo, turpentine, citrus from oranges, lemons, limes and grapefruit along with vegetables raised year-round, filled empty holds and carriages.

The lives of Winston and Octavia were much altered when they finally married and moved into the newly-built Rose Cottage on the banks of the babbling brook known locally as Acosta Creek. Their first child, Rosalie, was already toddling and talking. The next was on its way. The corn-crop was good, a raft of cypress trunks was being assembled to tow to Doctor May's mill, barrels of turpentine from slash-pine increased daily and kept the communal cooper busy at his craft and boxes of resin were filling to ship.

If trade continued.

"This is financial suicide," Octavia's father, during one of his rare appearances at a family function, repeated his oft quoted protests. "You can stockpile all the goods this great land can provide, but unless you can get it to market it will rot and you will starve."

"If the Yankees take our slaves, sir, we will starve anyway," Winston jounced his newly-christened daughter, Rosalie, on his crossed-over knee to play horsey, on the smoking-porch where Mother Bryant insisted the men take their smelly cigars.

That, also, echoed his planter's point of view.

Father Bryant, a grandfather again with the Welaka branch of his Florida family, petulantly flicked his cheroot ash.

"One of these days you, the South, is going to have to let go of this idea it is a divine right to own slaves and adjust, as the great civilized nations have. Not only is it morally wrong, but it is poor business," Winston's father-in-law insisted.

Before Winston could reply a distant cry of alarm rippled toward them. All eyes and a number of outstretched arms, pointed to a smoky cloud coming from the direction of Horse Landing, north-west across the river. If it was a brush-fire from a flared-up dormant lightening strike following a recent storm, it would burn itself out when it reached the marshes. But it could be the homestead and its extended jetty in peril.

The family affair broke up rapidly. The men mounted-up to ride north for a better view or ran to the boat dock, grabbing axes, buckets, blankets and a ladder, if needed to clamber onto a shingled-roof. Welaka's community, with its divergent stances, was of a singular mind where a neighbor's well-being was threatened. It could be them in need, next time.

"To be continued." Winston called over his shoulder, handing his daughter into his wife's care before unceremoniously vaulting over the rail to dash to his horse. Other members of his cavalry group were assembling too.

He smiled at the circumstance which had given the newly named St Johns Rangers an impromptu call-to-arms exercise. They were good lads and minded him well. He had heard of other formations which turned into chaos when the duly-elected officers based more on favoritism and beer bribes for 'good ole Joe' collapsed. Experience in the field trumped false figureheads, they soon realized. A set of skills could mean the difference between life and death if, and when, those messed-up exercises became actual combat situations.

Between the Bryant and Stephen families and surrounding neighbors, they knew their home territory well and would defend it to the death, if needs be. Winston was the only regular serving soldier. His men were mostly composed of farmers and fishermen clawing a living from the fickle land and seasonal whims. Drought, floods, freezes and brick-oven heat which could raise the temperature of metal enough to grill fish fillets, were uncontrollable elements which could wipe them out.

The fire they raced toward was fueled by pine-trees filled with the raw elements which they turned into turpentine to fuel lamps and stoves which extended their day, and heated their house and turned them into homes where families gathered, and could read books at the end of a winter day.

Crossing the creek which supplied Rose Cottage with potable water and drove the water-wheel which ground corn into grits, Winston drew closer to the smoke-clouds drifting eastward to put a pall over the land ahead. They heard and caught glimpses of the steam-launch *Juanita* heading down-river on an ebb-tide. Based on the rough terrain ahead and the curves in the river they would probably reach the site within minutes of each other.

Winston held his right hand up, then one finger. The group assembled into single-file, alphabetically just like they rehearsed, with no jostling for position. He cautiously guided them off the wagon-trail along deer-paths which could lead them to a fording area with a tiny beach where the shore bank was worn down from the hooves of many cloven creatures.

"Damn!" The expletive burst out, despite his promise to

Octavia.

"That's no lighting strike," his youthful brother in-law Henry cried. The boy reined his gray beside the Colonel. Others clustered about them.

The woods were intact, but the log homestead manned by Jesse Beaton and the ailing widow Ma Beaton, was fully engulfed. Flames had caught outbuildings, stables, pens and scrub-brush alight. The wind blew debris and sparks toward the rivers to sizzle and hiss, threatening the dock. There was no movement ashore except terrified horses and pigs.

"Quick. Cross over, cut back brush and use your blankets to smother anything landing on the dock. Form a bucket-line and let's see if we can save the livestock."

"What about the Beatons?"

"If they're alive, hopefully they've fled, Could be on the water somewhere. I don't see their raft," Winston called out.

He dismounted and walk-swam his horse into the river toward the other shore. The chug-chug of *Juanita* approached fast from upstream. He did not want to meet her mid-stream.

~~~

Jesse's charred remains were found, after the flames were doused by the combined efforts of militia, townsfolk and others who rallied to the distress tooting of *Juanita*'s steam-valve. Winston, as the highest-ranking official on the scene, made notes for a later report.

Jesse was found sprawled behind the back door of the cabin, while his mother's face-down body, was half-out of her bed. Her head at an odd-angle, barely attached to her body.

"Wildmen," the Colonel summarized once they walked through the building. Swep shot a look at him. "Remnants of the woodsmen sharing the wilderness with the Seminoles. Some are descended from each army who occupied Florida from the day it was found, some deserters from the Seminole Wars. They could have been escaping punishment for a misdeed, or just rogues. They could be pirates, privateers, buccaneers, runaway slaves of indentured servants." Winston rattled off the possibilities.

He patted the holster and the army-issued Colt he had retained from active service.

"Good reason to pack a firearm, wherever you go. Especially now, when your neighbor, or your brother-in-law could turn out to be your enemy," he joshed. It was said in sport, but they both recognized it was not far from the truth in their family, with Grandpa Bryant favoring the Union.

"Could have been a loner, tossed out of his own gang." Winston traded theories with Sanchez, the Cuban skipper of *Juanita*. "Better keep a watch where you tie-up for the night. He—they—are not likely to have traveled far on the raft. Looks like stores, tools, blankets were stripped out before it was set ablaze. Could be it was stolen to set up a homestead somewhere, a leanto somewhere in the woods, or to sell or trade,"

Sanchez nodded. "Those folks," he glanced at west-shore folks who clustered about. "They're gonna lose their supply deliveries if someone don't man this landing."

Winston the farmer and expeditor summed up the tasks ahead. "I'll tell'em. Give it time to sink in. Someone's going to have to bury them, do a service, contact next-of-kin, keep looters at bay and feed the livestock 'till it can be auctioned off if there's no claimants."

He called his brother over to select a couple of men to share the duty until the west-shore community or Swep could make arrangements.

Finally, before they shoved off by boat and horse, he addressed the civilians, outlined the circumstances, cautioned them to be aware and called upon them to select someone to maintain the supply stop.

"Another relaxing Sunday," he quipped as he leaned from his saddle to pat Swep on the shoulder in a parting gesture. "You be on the look-out, y'hear? And remember, the rockets are for emergencies – not entertainment!"

Swep gave him a broad-grin.

"What?"

"Thank you – for getting me out of tomorrow's chores. Think I'd rather be here than mucking-out the smoke-house sand," he said.

Winston smacked his forehead. Then smiled back.

"Burrel!" The slave's name burst from their lips in unison.

"He owes me. I gave him the time off to preach to his flock, today." Winston lowered his voice and head to confide to family. "And lent him my rifle to go hunt and sweeten the pot for their anniversary dinner, last week."

Swep's mouth turned down to accompany the slight shake of his head. "That's not good, Winnie."

Winston shrugged. "No one needs to know. Right?"

'Not from me, sir." The intimate moment flew in face of their relative ranks in the official world. They drew apart, to hold the ground while the Colonel led his troop home.

~~~

Juanita beat them to it and the community was already abuzz with stories of renegades, bandits and rogues wandering the land, in addition to the imminent arrival of Yankees and the freed slaves with vengeance in their black hearts.

Winston reminded his men, before dismissing them to return to their homes to team-up and cast more ammunition.

"I know the temptations to sling lead now the deer are fawning, and visiting the ripe new shoots of our crops," he grinned in empathy. "But let today serve as a reminder. That spent bullet, could be the one you need to save your life."

There were a couple of sheepish grins back and a lot of nodded heads.

"So?" he asked.

"So, we need some more ammo, sir," one sharp recruit led a chorus of responses.

Groans and laughter greeted the time-consuming task of melting lead, pouring it into molds then cutting or filing ridges and flanges excess to size.

~~~

The Bryant household, where some members of the Sunday party remained, included Octavia and little Rosalie.

There was additional activity, with the imminent departure of the head of the family. Stanley Bryant had been hinting for days he would head north, to Jacksonville and its settled, structured community.

"I'd rather take my chance there than risk being caught in the crossfire between a bunch of redneck hotheads slinging lead at anything that looks and sounds like a Yankee," he said.

Few tried to dissuade him. His absentee status, while annoying and burdensome to his wife and daughter, was preferable to the alternative fate which could befall him. Neighing horse clopping away, wagon-wheels squeaking under the weight of luggage and too many people, and calls of farewell drowned out distant rumblings in the air.

Dogs barked and horse-ears twitched.

"Early night storm?" Bryant asked.

"That's not nature's doing." Winston cocked his head, hearing the familiar distant methodical barrage of cannon-fire. "I think father Bryant will find his war has already arrived when he reaches his destination."

Mother Bryant overheard him. She crossed to reach for her husband's hand and squeezed it with a heart-felt pang of regret. Sadness that their imperfect partnership had kept them apart for so many years that they had missed sharing the joys of their family growing. Sorrow that their different upbringing, which had spiced the early years, should become a wedge dividing the family when unity was most needed.

He nodded. A tear rolled down his cheek to splash on her upturned face.

"We'll meet again," he said gently.

Rebecca fought back her own tears, straightened her back and smiled tightly.

"Take care of yourself, husband."

"I will. For you."

A crack of the whip and the carriage set off toward the river where the freshly stocked log-box held sufficient fuel to make the night run non-stop to Jacksonville.

Chapter 2

Crossing the Bar

The facade of southern hospitality displayed before the war in Florida's east coast port city of Jacksonville, disappeared with the prospect of immediate occupancy by Federal forces.

Merchantmen from the north, no matter their sympathies or neutrality, were in fear of their livelihood and lives, in the spring of 1862.

James Bryant, together with his in-laws and fellow Yankees formed a guard committee to patrol and keep watch over their properties. Most buildings were lined along a few blocks along the north-shore of the St. Johns. The so-called city, with a few hundred population, had access to the sea. Also it was the railroad junction between the east-west line between Fernandina on the Atlantic Ocean to the state capitol at Tallahassee, with a spur to Cedar Cay on the Gulf Coast.

Bryant and his fellow merchants found business brisk preceding the conflict and for the first few months when Confederate successes were in the ascent and popular talk spoke of a short war with a secessionist victory.

It peaked with the first ironclad assault by the Confederate ship *Virginia* when it rammed the sailing frigate USS *Cumberland* and sunk it in Hampton Roads. She then out fought the wooden USS *Columbia*'s guns whose cannon-balls could not penetrate the 5-inch iron shield.

The preponderance of Southerners from western Virginia, Alabama, the Carolinas and neighboring Georgia toed the secessionist-line or, at the very least, were socially ostracized. Firebrands in rhetoric and reality applied constant pressure on waverers, amongst their own kin. Yankees were fair game, targets for old scores to be settled in the name of patriotism. Given the opportunity, looting on a massive scale occurred before arsonists set to with pitch-soaked twig-bundles tossed into homes and storage areas.

Stories of Federalist attack and occupation of Fernandina, just miles north-east of the city, and a fleet of Union Navy ships filled with runaway slaves turned sailor under Federal freedom laws, sent ripples of fear and shock through Jacksonville.

"They'll be in here raping and pillaging," street-corner orators called, handing out hastily printed posters calling for: "the Righteous to gather at Church to receive The Word how to combat Satan's spawn and fight fire with fire." Refreshments provided by the kindness of the pastor's wife and his too many daughters.

Bryant and other merchants called their own meeting with less ballyhoo, in the backroom of Calvin Robinson's hardware store and sawmill. For weeks, during the unflagging ferrying of goods upon the St. Johns perpetually flowing waters, all but display items were removed from premises open to the public to shop, and sealed warehouses limited to staff. A fall-back location across the river on the western shore a little south of what used to be where cattle forded the river had been quietly established.

"We have to evacuate the women and children by boat, before it's too later," Robinson urged.

"It's dangerous out there. It's a wilderness teeming with creatures and hostiles," cried one shopkeeper. The term covered everything from bandits to natives and runaway slaves.

"There might be a few undesirables roaming," the merchant admitted. "But armed and supplied, we're more than a match for them."

A church bell rang in the distance, calling the faithful to prayer and meeting.

"These are the people we need to fear. The righteous, God-fearing zealots too blinded by hatred to listen to reason. They will pray for our souls, after they have ripped the life out of our bodies," the Yankee matched the passion displayed by his southern neighbors.

Juanita was due to arrive later that day. Secretly Bryant's fellow northerners, in ones and twos with their children gathered at his store headquarters. A small group of row-boats from dinghies to ship's cutters pressed into service to ferry supplies from ship to ship, assembled at his jetties.

Long after the sun set, *Juanita*'s crew rowed her with muffled oars into the rising river with a string of smaller boats, also rowed, attached to each other by bow and stern-lines like so many pearls on a chain. Once down river and out of rifle-shot, *Juanita*'s primed engine was thrust into gear.

In the dark cloudy night with the hint of a spring shower, the silent convoy of refugees in their own land fled their fellow countrymen, for sanctuary in Florida's wilderness beset by creatures of the night and unknown human predators.

It was late in the day before their absence was discovered. The customers who showed up to buy what meager supplies still graced the wooden shelves and display-stands, found all doors locked. Save one, where Calvin Robinson stood his ground. Logic told him he and his enterprise would be spared the wrath of his turncoat southern neighbors when they realized he was their only source of sustenance.

He was mistaken.

While the Watch Committee was still meeting that evening, and the gunfire of Union ships gathering at the mouth of the St. Johns could be heard rumbling in the air, renegades took matters into their own hands. And whatever they could haul away, as well, before setting everything they did not own ablaze.

Only when the wind shifted and flying embers began to waft onto roofs of the residential areas, did any attempt to dampen the fire-storm, begin.

"Reap what you sow," a merchant observer said. He wiped away tears, having watched the conflagration through a telescope from across the river.

"Amen" chorused those within hearing. Watching their hard-fought livelihood consumed before their eyes, with slim prospects of survival in their current situation, even the most pacifist person there had the spark of anger and revenge fanned into flame from what they observed.

~~~

The local authorities from the mayor down tried to save the town.

Confederate authorities faced a difficult choice.

If Union forces crossed the bar and had access to waters bordering Jacksonville, there were no cannons to resist and the motley militia could not be relied upon to lay down their lives to save the munitions and fuel depot: neither the converted tow-boat nor the newly arrived schooner, *America*.

They could initiate a scorched-earth tactic from which there would be no recovery for them, but no rewards for the enemy.

Or, cut and run to fight another day.

The railway offered an out.

Its link to Fernandina was destroyed, but its route north and west was still operable. The Confederate gunboat on the hard, useless with a blown boiler, would have to be sacrificed, but the world's fastest schooner could be saved if drastic, secret action was taken swiftly.

Chapter 3

The Hunt

It was only a glimpse in the final seconds of twilight, but Sam swore he saw the schooner of his childhood silhouetted against the last light of the day, all sails flying, headed for enemy territory.

He was aboard the steam gunboat *USS Ottawa* patrolling waters between Fernandina and Jacksonville inlets, following one of the more bizarre encounters of the war; a ship chasing a train, when the specter of *America* passed before his eyes.

Sambuca was at the head tending to his business, like the rest of the crew did, when he yowled in a most plaintive way. His back arched and the hair stood up along the ridge, just as the hairs on Sam's neck tingled.

"Ship ahoy, dammit." His voice carried to the helmsman, the bridge and aloft to the sunset-gazing lookout whose view of the western horizon, higher up the mast, was a turmoil of red and gold-tinged clouds gradually fading to gray then black.

Sam darted back to the bridge, ascended and pointed toward the wraith.

"Are you sure?" Lt. Thomas Holdup Stevens had also gained the bridge from his cabin below.

"Seems impossible, sir, but I'd swear a month's pay she was the old yacht *America*," the ship's navigation and executive officer called from the landward end of the bridge.

Lt. Samuel Taylor peered intently through a newly acquired set of binoculars, seized from the duty signalman. Not as powerful as the captain's telescope, they offered a wider field of vision.

The last glimmer of twilight vanished as quickly as a velvet curtain pulled across a bay-window.

Nothing but a few isolated homestead lights dotted the barrier-island shoreline. No moon shone on the muddy inlet waters flowing from the mouth of St. Johns River, that night. No signs of fisherman's lanterns bobbing on the waters luring fish into casting-nets. The presence of Union ships patrolling off-shore had honest and hostile citizens hugging the shoreline, surf-casting or turtle-egg hunting, to fill the pot and their bellies.

"Make a note in the log," Stevens instructed. "Once we are south of the inlet we'll head off-shore, haul the rags and heave-to. Tell the engineer to keep up steam, though. I'm going to finish my supper."

Lt. Stevens' confidence in the younger man was reflected in the casual handing back of command of the deck

"Aye, aye sir," Sam replied.

He snapped off a formal salute for the sake of other ranks who never missed a bit of gossip to natter about. The crew was as quick to grumble about discipline as they were about lackadaisical officers. As a hawser-rat, one of the nicer expletives assigned to officers who had made their way from the fo'c'sle to the quarterdeck, he was acutely aware of mess-deck mentality.

Sam's arrival aboard the '90-day gunboat', as the hastily built Unadilla-class *USS Ottowa* schooner was called, complete with cat in the fall of 1891, supplied grist to the gossip mill. His slightly bent posture, due to his six-foot plus height and the ship's standard deck-height of six-foot, plus a leprechaun peach-fuzz beard, reminded many of Washington Irving's, Icabod Crane. But, sailors from the Sandy Hook shore, familiar with some of the legendary antics of competitive pilots with their brawls at sea and ashore to settle old score, doubted he would shy away from a challenge.

~~~

"What's that damned cat doing here? Get it off."

"He goes, I go. Sir," piped up the lanky new arrival that scrambled aboard from the lugger bringing supplies and personnel aboard the moored gun-boat.

Sam attempted to salute the flag, hang on to his portmanteau, acknowledge the officer of the watch and coax the inquisitive Samubco within reach. It was a familiar issue faced at other commands since he had been seconded to the hastily assembled new Union Navy, and newly activated irregular volunteer commissioned officers. The desperate shortage of ships and sailors to handle them with officers to lead following the creation of the Atlantic Blockading Squadron, called for some compromises. The social niceties and customs of the old regulars, raised within the closed ranks of the gun-room and quarterdeck, were waived in favor of manpower.

Lt. Vincent was speechless. He had not faced such impudence during a career spanning decades. His face turned purple, fists clenching, aware he was the focus of all eyes on deck.

The next step, a source of much speculation amongst the crew, was prevented by a hail from the bridge by the captain.

"Welcome aboard, stow your gear below and report to me. Lets clear the way now, we have men and supplies waiting to board." Lt. Stevens called from his perch on the exposed iron-bridge before *Ottawa*'s tall black smokestack.

Sam edged his way past the spluttering deck officer, aft, instinctively heading for officer territory. A mess-steward who had held back to watch the fireworks, stepped forward to scoop the new officer's belongings and guide him below.

"Sambuca."

The errant cat escaped the clutches of a seaman who

cradled him to dart after Sam's call.

A muffled sneeze from the gangway raised a smile. There was a reason, other than superstition, causing the duty officer to object to a black cat joining the ship.

During *Ottowa*'s workup sea-trials the middle-aged captain, latest in a series of seafaring line to serve aboard fighting ships, grew to rely on the beanpole navigator-pilot wished upon him. He was socially deferential but insistent in all matters concerning tide, time and place. Beyond the tools of navigation, he could read water, sky and wind to plot a course which would get *Ottawa,* under sail, where she needed to be before others in the squadron who succumbed to the temptation to compete.

Sam accompanied Stevens and the still-rankled Vincent, to a squadron meeting following completion of sea-trials, for their first fleet maneuver. The strategy of blockading and undermining secessionist states ability to combat union forces, without imposing irreparable damage and loss of life on either side, would require skill, and guile.

"The street-corner rabble-rousers and propagandists found in the newly illustrated magazines are as much our enemy as he who wields a sword or fires a gun. Perhaps more so," the speaker, Captain Samuel DuPont stood before a map of the Atlantic and Gulf coasts, bordered far to the west by the straggling Mississippi river. He held a handful of weekly published pictorial papers. Some depicted federalist troops raiding, pillaging and burning mansions in the south. Others showed intermingling of black and white races with southern belles cavorting in splendid ballrooms in the arms of former slaves while white men watched impotently.

"They dredge stories up of the slime of the slave overthrow of their French masters in Santa Domingo, and the massacre of whites in Haiti. That is not going to happen, here. As we move into the secessionists' states and tighten our grip on its lifeline, we will also be recruiting from the ranks of freedmen and escapees, as the case may be." A ripple of comments all but drowned out his further remarks.

"Don't believe what you read in the papers." DuPont's deep voice rose above the background. "Remember that one about 'We can take on the Yankees, ten to one.' and 'Blacks can't fight'. We have all served aboard ships with mixed crews in every navy under the sun. If a man cannot carry his weight he is taught, one way or another, to do so."

He smacked a fist into his cupped hand with a resounding thwack.

There were a few nervous chuckles from line-officers who recalled the boson's knotted-rope starters to persuade sailors slow to climb aloft, or put their weight behind the bar of a windlass to weigh anchor. The lash, applied to backs bared to a cat-o-nine-tails, created many a scar on seasoned sailors of the old navy.

Part of the strategy which would serve to undermine the south, and swell the ranks of a navy which only had 46 active vessels on its roster before the first shots were fired in anger, would be to retain and not return runaways, known as 'contraband'. Before hostilities, slave owners could demand return of slaves smuggled into free-states, if they could find them. Posters with woodcut images, a description of clothing and capabilities they had been taught; for house or field service, were distributed by agents offering rewards. Bounty hunters were dispatched to handle recalcitrant abolitionist employers.

"Most will need to be trained, just like the old colonial press-ganged recruits. But, we're good at that, eh?" DuPont's wry comment raised a few grimaces from those who recalled stories behind the cause of the war of 1812. "But there is no cause for alarm aboard, or ashore. They may not be like us," his glance swept the room of white faces above blue uniforms," but they are able-bodied men capable of being good crew. They know the consequences of failure."

In an age of steam ships and iron-bound hulls, secure fueling sources for the coal needed to drive the war machines, had to be established. No longer could navies roam the world powered by the wind, relying on salt-pork, hard-tack , water, rum and lime to keep crews fighting fit. DuPont's chart showed potential bases.

Three locations were circled: Port Royal, South Carolina, with its deep sound and defensible site; Fernandina, between Cumberland Sound at the St. Mary's River border of Florida with Georgia on St. Amelia Island, and the abandoned brick-built Fort Clinch; and St Augustine, oldest city in America with its confederate-held Spanish fort, surrounded by a polyglot population favoring the union.

Following the meeting Sam joined others scrutinizing the chart and making notes. The cedar-sheathed lead-pencil which lightly traced the railway tracks from the Atlantic to the Gulf coast, may have begun life as a tree on Cedar Cay. But his eyes dropped to the confusing mess of lines and figures surrounding the entrance to the St. Johns River, which gave access to the city of Jacksonville.

"That's going to be interesting." He tapped the chart. Stevens and Vincent glanced at him."The shape of the channel and depth of the sandbar constantly changes. We draw nine-feet, on a good day. It's going to be skinny and risky getting in there, without a pilot."

"I thought you were a pilot," Vincent sneered,

"Sandy Hook and New York, sir," Sam reminded him. "It'll take a while to read this entrance. Chances are, it won't be a picnic survey, with sharpshooters taking pot-shots at the pinnace."

"So, go in at night," Steven lightly suggested. Vincent flinched but Sam smiled.

"Great minds, sir. I should be able to get a bearing, once we've established shore-light sources. A good leads-man should have no problem reading the line. I'll begin a blind-fold course, tomorrow." He turned to Vincent. "Care to make a wager? Port or starboard watch?"

The senior lieutenant's eyes lit up with the first show of

interest he had shown all night.

Stevens said nothing but made a mental note that his newly arrived officer had quickly assessed Vincent, and tapped into the scuttlebutt source of stories. It was as well to keep a thumb on the pulse of the ship for other, less trivial early warnings. Trouble-makers and lower-deck lawyers liked the sound of their own voices too much to keep many secrets aboard a ship, if one knew how to tap into the source.

"Once we secure Port Royal..."Stevens began.

"...and capture Fernandina," Vincent concluded.

Chapter 4

The Chase

Capture of Port Royal during the early days of March, 1862, was a bloodless affair.

When the fleet of Union ships appeared the occupants of the port fled further inland, leaving the deep-water port free for occupancy. The confederate troops who had been assembled there earlier had been withdrawn to join other Florida soldiers in the Confederate Western Theater near the vital supply route provided by the Mississippi River.

Once DuPont's naval elements established a foothold and colliers from the north began delivering tons of coal essential to conduct a steam-ship war, the Union ships including *Ottawa* could continue their voyage of occupation southward, into Florida.

The white sugar-sand shoreline beyond the gray-green sea rolling in to break on the beach, was stained brown from tannin leaching into inland waterways, rivers and streams from the dense forests of pine and oak growing along their banks. Fernandina's much occupied community; it grew up under seven flags of established nations as well as buccaneers, pirates and freebooters in times of dispute, offered scant resistance from the earthenware ramparts of Fort Clinch, strategically situated near the river.

Once the token force walked into the deserted fort, the reason became apparent.

"The greybacks have made a run for it, and loaded up aboard the train for Jacksonville and inland," a messenger called out from a pinnace headed toward the fleet-commander's ship. A slave in homespun clothes who stood alongside him, vigorously nodded his head. "They're all at the station."

Sam's alert eyes had steered *Ottawa* clear of a hulk, hastily sunken to hamper their progress. A swirl of water above the submerged vessel, different from the flow of the ebbing tide, warned him. His ship's change of course was followed by the line of vessels following in its wake. His finger traced the skimpy rough-drawn map, their only guide to the land ahead. Neat blocks of residential streets, with the mercantile warehouses, community center for market and jail, including the rail-head terminal.

"Captain," he called from his perch in the ratlines supporting the forward mast."I can see the rail bridge and a train from the town approaching it. It runs along the Amelia Island riverbank. There's good water..."

"Follow his finger," the spontaneous response from Stevens, flummoxed the helmsman for a second before, grinning, he turn the wheel a notch or so, A call down the brass voice-pipe from bridge to engine-room, was more measured and nautical.

"Give me full-speed ahead, Chief."

Below deck the engineer and his crew stared blank-faced through coal-grimed red-rimmed eyes. Their creeping progress into enemy-held territory was nerve-wracking enough. But the new orders exceeded their expectations.

"We're chasing a train, chief,"Stevens gleefully called down. "That's one to tell your grandchildren, eh?"

"Bludy maniaces."

The chief's response echoed his brethren's contempt for sailors in general, and captain's demanding the impossible, in particular. His mates and close-knit stoker-crew nodded agreement. When the ship's complement was not fighting other ships ashore, they would as easily get into it with other branches aboard.

Ottawa's slim black bow thrust a brown mustache wave, which sent small tenders and fisherman's boats rocking at their moorings and boats tied alongside jetties squeaking and tugging against shore-lines, when the broad-bladed propeller blades bit deep and faster to froth the water under her stern.

The chase was on.

~~~

The last train from Fernandina sluggishly jerked away from the confines of the city beneath its seventh flag, that of the newly-formed Confederate nation.

It made no difference to engineer Thaddy Popkin who occupied it, as long as his New York masters paid his wages. He glanced at the gauges, tapped the glass on one, then peered ahead at the parallel iron rail curving with the contour of the river-bank. His fireman slammed the furnace door closed, ran a tattooed arm across his dripping brow, crossed the cab and stuck his head into the onrush of air.

He barely noticed the panorama of green marshes across the mirrored sky of the bay on the waters, the ripples and splashes of mullet running and leaping ahead of an unseen predator, sand-cranes stalking the shallows or an anhinger perched on a branch drying its wings. But, when he turned inward to make a comment, his eyes took in a most unexpected sight.

There was an armed gunboat, black smoke billowing from its tall funnel, pursuing them with a cluster of men on the bow surrounding a cannon. Pointed at him.

That's when he noticed the red-white and blue of the Union flag flapping from the halliard, aft.

"Chief," he called out, "we gots us a Yankee gunboat up our ass."

Passengers, crammed into the carriages, had also noticed their pursuer. Between civilians, children, household pets, luggage cramming every available space, the armed soldiers were hard-pressed to possess spots at the railway-carriage windows to form any sort of defense. Some younger civilians gleefully pushed through the crowd toward the last car, armed with hunting muskets and a couple of hand-guns.

Those aboard *Ottawa* could see the closing target chugging along a two-mile stretch of track before the bridge carried the rail into the woods on the mainland.

"Come on chief. Give us all you've got." Stevens cupped his hands around the mouthpiece to bellow below. The deck shook beneath him, stacked cutlasses rattled in the ready-racks. The ship's side was crowded with crew, all leaning forward as though to urge the ship forward, faster. The water ahead erupted into tiny fountains where shots from the baggage-car were being fired at them.

"Take cover boys. It just needs one lucky shot."

The boson crouched his way crab-like forward, pressing the heads of curious and excited sailors down, behind the bulwark. Cannon poked out from ports if there was an opportunity for a broadside.

The gun-crew had little to hide behind, exposed on the open foredeck.

Ottawa's bow thrust forward faster after the engineer tweaked the safety valve to direct a few extra pounds of steam into her new engines. Conversation below was limited to hand-signals. Several members of the black-gang as the stokers were called – among other things – copied his movements when he crossed himself.

Sambuca settled himself on the cross-trees, curiously watching the world about him. Sam had the best but most vulnerable location aboard. The wobbling train, partially obscured under a cloud of pungent smoke streaming back from the straining engine, was bristling with the muzzles of guns poking through opened windows. A trestle bridge straddled a stream separating the island to the mainland lay less than a mile ahead. His eyes swung down to the waters ahead. He could see the flow from under the bridge and a small bar extending from the shore before darker water indicated the seaward channel.

Beyond the stream, dark-brown water turned to yellow where the undisturbed shoreline and marsh-grasses claimed ownership between stands of cypress trees with underwater roots. Spanish moss extended in a canopy into the shadowed forests behind, and draped toward the water's surface.

"Fire when ready." Stevens' gale-force order, amplified by a speaker-trumpet, was all the encouragement Lt. Vincent and his crew needed.

Sambuca's tail twitched. He yowled, stood and arched his back, staring at the target, Sam said later.

The first 11-inch shell from the soda-bottle shaped Dahlgren bow-gun exploded in a fiery blast, cordite fumes wafted back to fill the nostrils of all who watched eagerly for its point of impact.

A mighty splash soaked passengers in the third carriage from the end. Cheers and groans rose from the deck of *Ottawa*.

"Fire!"

A second shot exploded a hundred yards into the track behind the fleeing train. Several celebratory shots were fired from the fleeing train and a taunting rebel-yell drifted back across the water.

"Third time lucky, lads." An older gunner called from the waist, taking the unlit clay pipe out of a toothless mouth.

So it proved.

The baggage car jerked and slewed across the tracks like a dragging anchor, chewing up the ground beneath, and slowing progress of the straining engine. For a moment, watching the wobbling carriages, it looked as though the first encounter between a ship and train would chalk up a victory for the navy.

Troops poured out of the stalled train carriages, knelt and sent a withering fusillade toward *Ottawa* peppering the waters into a lethal froth before her bow.

Her exposed gun-crew held station but anxiously

looked aft at the bridge.

Captain Stevens surveyed the situation. The getaway train was shielded far ahead of the stalled carriages, most of which were also across the bridge, except for the last one, derailed and swarming with a hornet's nest of angry rebels spitting fire.

There were far too many defending troops ashore to attempt an assault. The rest of the fleet, sirens blasting at the delaying shot, were strung out far astern. Rebel troops were uncoupling the chain of carriages, emptying what stores they could and evacuating killed and wounded out of sight to awaiting hands.

"Half-speed. Wheel port, ten degrees. Load with grapeshot."

The order pulled *Ottawa* away from the shore which would present a larger target for his enemy; but a broadside of flying lead spraying the recovery team should keep their heads – and weapons – down.

In the event that parting shot was never made.

A double-toot from the hidden engine and the slow, jerky, forward movement of the train's last occupied carriage, plus abandonment of the overturned car, signaled the lurching retreat of Confederate forces from Fernandina.

"Three short blasts." Stevens ordered a sporting breaking off the engagement.

A corresponding response, from the direction of the oily-black smoke rising from a mass of treetops stretching as far as the eye could encompass, signaled a thankful farewell and acknowledgment, from their foe.

Chapter 5

Assault

Word of Fernadina's fall and the approaching Federal fleet was carried to Jacksonville by evacuees arriving on that last, troop-filled train.

Word of mouth embellished the horrors of ruthless invaders who had set the slaves free to run amok amongst the sainted citizens, plundering, looting and other acts too ghastly to relate. Fears of slave uprisings, similar to those experienced by French plantation owners and white citizens of Haiti, slaughtered by savages, spread from fence to fence throughout the city. More carriages were added to the troop train for citizens fleeing west.

Militia groups bid farewell to their families, milling about waiting for orders. Some senior, soothing heads, urged calming anxieties and a delegation of known Union sympathizers to meet and greet any federal leaders who were able to pass through fire from Fort Steele protecting St. Johns River, if they could cross the bar.

Others, more virulent and possibly motivated by a little private payback and pillaging, took matters into their own hands.

"Leave nothing for the Yankees. Burn, burn, burn."

Groups armed with pitch-torches paraded along waterfront warehouses timber yards and toward docks and boat-yard where a newly-built 50-foot, 600-ton Confederate two-engined schooner-rigged gunboat-hull, stood propped up on the hard.

Beyond it the steamer *St. Mary*, boilers fired, stood by the docked schooner *America*, warily watching the flare of torches stringing along the waterfront, edging closer.

Under the frightful light of flames reflected upon the river waters, *Juanita* warily held her own against the rising tide, sticking to the shadows. The noise of her engine submerged under the roar of flames, occasional explosions of wood and merchandise mingling with the tumult of the crowd. The launch made for a small knoll where the last holdout Yankee trader, a few possessions and those loyal employees who remained sat helplessly in the row-boat they had hoped to escape in.

The oars had been turfed into the flowing waters to drift out of reach, south with the tide, by a malicious vagabond, unable to turn them into profit. The anchor, chain and line were missing, too.

Merchant Robinson, the last holdout, emerged from the scrub-land scarred from a cluster of Spanish bayonet plants where he'd buried his money pots. He saw the outline of *Juanita* edging toward them. He waved frantically, peering back over his shoulder toward sounds of the liquored-up mob rampaging a mere block away, heading toward the boatyard.

"Cast off." He called out. "Paddle with your hands, deck-boards, anything, Get us away from this Hades created by heathens."

The two light lines holding the overcrowded boat to land were untied and pulled aboard, while a series of splashes from desperate men, and squeals from sprayed children scared but excited by the adventure, traced the slow withdrawal of the last Yankee boat to lave Jacksonville.

The last Confederate ships also pulled away from shore and the threat of fiery destruction, just a few hundred yards further along the waterfront. *St. Mary*'s engines picked up the tempo, carried by the tide away from land, with her towline barely taut dripping water back into the river while the bowsprit of *America* followed in her wake. Few saw the departure of the iconic vessel make her escape.

Few thought they would see her again. That included *Juanita*'s skipper. His eyes swung away from the historic spectacle to his own drama unfolding with the safe contact between the launch and rowboat secured alongside, with her cargo of refugees, wet, cold and subdued in the chill night air away from the conflagration which had been their home. Yesterday's anxiety and fear for the future had become an unforgettable reality.

~~~

Jacksonville's whereabouts was plain to distinguish in the dark mass of land west of the mouth of the St. Johns River. Scarlet skies reflecting flames billowing below low clouds and tumbling smoke rising to blend into them, were a beacon beckoning the stalled fleet impatient to meet the enemy.

Sam's nighttime practice with his chosen leads-men provided a critical cog in the war machine of occupation. During the preceding days *Ottawa* cruised closer into the mouth of awaiting Confederates of unknown quantity within Jacksonville, and the garrison stationed within the walls of Fort Steele. From high above, perched on mast or wrapped around ratlines supporting them, he read the swirling waters ebbing from the muddy river.

Smooth patches, races, disturbances, all reflected the contour of what lay below the surface. His team plumbed those areas during that brief slack water period between ebb and flood, being careful to remain out of range from musket-balls sent their way from sharp shooters ashore. Though the old-fashioned muskets being used by rebels were mostly of the muzzle-loading variety, there was little scorn expressed of their accuracy.

"Don't make no mind if it takes one or five minutes, between shots, if the one that blowed your brains out finds it mark, do it?" An old salt chided a sharpshooter marine, lovingly oiling his newly-issued single-shot Sharps carbine, which could be loaded and fired at the breech within less than

10-seconds.

With the early dark of March, a moonless night, a slack-tide and a couple of boat-loads of leads-men reading the bottom and noting their finding on hand-drawn charts provided by Sam, the obstacles they faced to cross the bar quickly became apparent.

"Our first choice would be to follow this course," his finger traced a path favoring the shore, under the deck-light hanging over Lt. Stevens' cabin desk. Scraps of paper, odd maps and charts lay atop the official survey taken a decade earlier when the US Navy relied on local pilots to guide ships safely to shore.

"But...?"

"But, sir, that would take us too close to batteries ashore. That we know of. There could be others concealed from sight..."

"We would only discover them when they open fire." Steven's concluded. "And so..."

"I'd suggest, sir, we await full flood, pray for an onshore wind, catch a wave and force our way through here."

Lt. Vincent gasped. Marine Captain Wilson grimaced; whether from the wardroom victuals or audaciousness of the reserve-officer's proposal was uncertain. Stevens pursed his lips, cocked his head and squinted at the labyrinth of penciled lines, dotted, broken and straight, lightly marked on the chart.

"How long before high tide?"

"Barely three hours." The ship's master contributed.

"What are we drawing?"

"Right at nine feet, sir."

"What have we got in the bilges?"

"A tad over a foot, I reckon."

"Reckoning's not good enough. I want those bilges bone-dry so I can pour salt on 'em – and pick it up to sprinkle again. Understood?"

"Aye, aye, sir." There could be no other response.

"Let us pass the word. We'll use the *Ellen* to store

whatever unnecessary materials we have aboard. She can do the same for the rest of the squadron." He rattled off orders which would allow the old New York ferry-boat to play an active-role in the conflict ahead, without putting its civilian crew in harms way.

"Anything else, sir?"

"Yes chief. Instruct ships-company to take a visit to the head before we go into action. That should lighten ship by a few tons – and avoid any embarrassing displays from new recruits, eh?" His irreverent comment sent his team about its work with a smile on their faces.

The pile of papers on his desk heaved. Sambuca's blue eyes peered up at him, unblinking.

"I could have you shot as a spy. You realize that, don't you."

The captain reached out a hand to scratch the cat's head. It arched its back, sending papers tumbling to the cabin floor and began to purr.

Part V

Home front

Chapter 1

Home front

"What am I going to do?" Penelope Hooten wailed. "The minister has enlisted along with the vestrymen. Who's going to christen my Timothy?"

It was the latest crises Tivie and her mother faced amongst members of Welaka Ladies Confederate Sewing Circle during the second year of the schism between south and north. Most of the menfolk, from boys to grandfathers had volunteered or been shamed into enlisting. Those same patriots, months later, finally realized the inflated enthusiasm which forecast a short conflict, had sadly erred in the resolve of both sides to press on.

"Now, don't take on so, Miss Penelope." Rebecca set aside the colorful swatch of scrape cloth she was cutting for her quilt, to pat the knee beneath the heavy homespun skirt the young mother wore. The child in question had suckled and been set aside with the other babes accompanying their mothers.

Cries and squeals of older children no longer confined behind school-desks; their teachers had also left to be trained as soldiers, rang out through the thin sheets of glass distorted by bubbles. No ball games were allowed near the house for fear the precious panes would be shattered. The ladies needed all the God-given light the day could provide to do their war-work, sewing uniforms, knitting socks and compiling comforters for hospitalized patients. Once the night clouds rolled in, firelight and whatever wax-based lighting available, was pressed into service. The oil-lamps of old had long since run dry, along with many items they took for granted, before the blockade began.

"We can hold it at Rose Cottage," Tivie said.

"How?" Rebecca swung her head toward her daughter. Really, the girl was becoming very bossy ever since Winston had left with his troop to bivouac as sentinels at Bison Bluff. Their role, to warn the community of any advancing Union invaders, could have been left to any of the boys tending the fields, in Mother Bryant's reckoning.

"But mother, they would run away to join the Yankees, or forget what they were supposed to do,"Tivie had crossly replied.

"Not if they knew they'd get to feel the switch, in my hand." Rebecca demonstrated with a flourish.

That waste of time argument was one of many mother and daughter had during the months both families lived under the same roof at Rose Cottage, following the scare earlier when unknown marauders swept through the tiny township one night, and absconded with pigs, chickens, eggs and precious salt from the smoke house. No one was aware until the following morning. But fear ratcheted up several notches of what could have been, if the thieves had been challenged or had broken into houses.

"Burrel can do it," Tivie said.

"The niggra?

"Why not? He's a practicing preacher of the Bible. Many of us have attended his Sunday services. Our children play with his children. He knows the words. And he's here." Tivie ticked off her points on fingers tender from needle-pricks acquired during her sewing sessions.

The chatter in the room died. An informal social gathering of neighbors with a common purpose had taken an unexpected turn.

Few held slaves of their own. Some leased or hired them for short-term tasks. Most aspired to become planters.

Wealthy planters, whose colonnaded mansions they recalled from their home states south of the Mason-Dixon line where most of them hailed from. They knew there was less chance of achieving that than spit surviving on a hot skillet, but it inspired some to get up before dawn to tend their homesteaded land, wresting arable land from forest and undergrowth to raise crops.

"But he's a slave."

"And our last Pastor was a shingle-maker," Rebecca readily responded in her daughter's defense. "Who do you think worked harder?"

Her smile lessened the rebuke, raising a few titters.

"He won't be preaching. Just repeating the Word."

"But he can read." Scolded a stout thin-lipped matron, whose black ensemble resembled the latest engraving in *Leslie's Weekly Magazine* of England's Queen Victoria. That dog-eared edition had passed through the hands of all present, as had magazines and books exchanged in an honor-system informal library they had established when the normal flow of publications were cut off.

"Just as well, too." Ellie Thompson chirped in."He taught his missus who tends my young 'uns, and she's taught them their A,B,C's."

"Mine too," a few other voices joined in.

In the silence which followed the sounds of exuberant children, black and white playing together outside flowed into the room, drowning out the constant clicking of needles knitting socks and scarves for soldiers far from home.

"*Extremis malis, extrema remedia.*" Octavia quoted a recalled phrase from her Yankee school, usually accompanied by an eye-roll from a teacher who had briskly applied a wooden ruler to the knuckles of a miscreant pupil. "Desperate times call for desperate measures," she loosely translated to the ring of blank faces staring at her.

Her mother smiled.

"Then that's settled." Her authorative voice interjected

before any further discussion interupted the sewing circle. "I have a treat for you all. Missie," she called toward the kitchen.

A few moments later the big bottomed house servant squeezed between the circle of chairs and ornately inlaid mahogany and cherrywood sideboard, to place a punch-bowl filled with cream nectar. The wartime substitute for mint julep and sherry cobbler, was painstakingly created using various fruits grown or wild, gathered, placed in a jar to ferment with whatever sugar or honey could be gathered. The end-result gave a little fillip at the conclusion of their sessions.

"I swear, those proper church ladies would never grace my door if it wasn't for the chance of something to tickle their palates," Rebecca muttered before each session.

The ladies, some a little wobbly, departed with their children soon after the punch-bowl emptied. Little alliances would exchange observations and gossip with neighbors before the next session, when a veneer of civility would conceal to the casual observer the rifts between them.

~~~

The familiar rumble of a side-wheeler engine cut through the crisp air before dawn. Men curled in the fetal position bundled up in blankets stirred in their slumber, ears anticipating an order which would rouse them to enter the March morning of mist.

It didn't come.

Instead, silence returned to the bivouac area of Bison's Bluff after a series of changes in engine pitch and pauses during forward and aft motion of the tug-boat wheels.

Winston chewed on the soggy, unlit, cheroot waiting for his scout to return from the source of the interruption.

"I reckon its Dunn's Creek way. Could be Murphy or Rat."

His brother's acute hearing and sharp eyesight were a blessing and a curse to the younger Stephens' boy. Tracking wildlife was as easy as reading the good book to a Sunday-school Bible study group. But the blast of musket-fire set his ears and head ringing for minutes on end. His only protection against the noise was to thrust his fingers in his ears.

"Then I'd have to take my boots off and use my toes," he'd joke.

Swep's estimate of the noise source, in the direction of two islands guarding the entrance to Dunn's Creek and its meandering path to Crescent Lake, proved correct.. It did not take him long to forge through undergrowth along a deer path with his stout cow-pony. The stocky creature, low on looks compared to high-stepping carriage trotters, could force a herd of cattle to follow a direction his cracker-rider selected. The flick of a herdsman's10-foot rawhide whip which snapped at its tip, cracking above the ear of any errant cow, also kept the bovine on course.

What he saw, from the concealment of and growth overlooking the watery junction of islands and mainland, was a puzzler.

A fine-looking black-hulled schooner with the gilt-letter name *Camilla* on her transom was being towed to the south-east side of Rat Island by the steamboat *St. Mary;* a familiar sight at Palatka on her frequent delivery runs from Jacksonville.

"There was a lot of commotion aboard both." Swep reported to Winston. The faces of his men never lifted from their plates of pork and grits, but the lack of breakfast chatter indicated all ears were tuned to the Bryant brothers.

"They was arguing, seem to me, 'bout whether to chop her masts down, then scuttle her."

"And?"

"They run lines off her starboard side to the steamer, and from her mast-tops to *Rat Island* cypress bases at the waterline. They must've holed her. She started to settle in the water. Teams hauled the lines like she was being careened – in about twenty foot of water, I guess." He held his arm upright then lowered it toward the ground, demonstrating the masts dipping down.

Most of Winston's troops were familiar with the islands and waters being described. In their mind's eye they could picture the scene.

"Once her deck reached the water it just poured onto the opened hatches and she slipped below, quick as that," clicked his finger and thumb.

"What happened to the crew? Are they ashore?" Winston asked.

"Wasn't much crew on the schooner, just that old Limey from Jacksonville, old man Hamming and his boy Charlie."

Winston nodded. Most everyone on the river knew of the flamboyant English purser of the steamboat *Welaka*, and his dual roles as a city mover and shaker wherever there was a dollar to be turned, including house and cattle auctioneer.

The men of East Putnam, all locals, fathers, sons, brothers, cousins, knew their territory well. They could relate to the lay of the land, the depth of the water, tidal action and best spots to cast a line for the fish they fancied; for the plate or fun. The northern flow of water from Crescent lake had gouged out a trough favoring the Rat Island side of Dunn's Creek. There was little land rise above high-tide which pushed its way that far south until the middle portion of the island, and that was cleft into a ragged, overgrown ravine maybe a dozen feet deep. A pool of fresh water, fed by aquifer layers underneath the land, supported the island's wildlife and nomads who roamed the state scrounging a living.

Once again the twittering and chirping background and occasional snort from a cobbled horse, was interrupted by steam venting and churning paddle-wheels approaching the bluff.

"She's headed south." stated the obvious.

"To Lake George or Crescent?" Winston wondered aloud.

All strained to hear any change to indicate the unseen but audible ship would employ one paddle over the other to turn to Port from the St. Johns onto the route east toward Crescent Lake toward the coast, or deeper south. The thrumbing of paddles and churned water seemed to flood in, filtering through the trees

"Well, she sure ain't going back to Jax," a pipe-sucking vet of the Seminole Wars, drawled. "Could be, she's running ahead of the Feds and dumped her tow."

His estimate was not far from the steamboat captain's plan. But deep water, enough to scuttle and conceal *St. Mary* from any pursuing Union vessel and deny them her use, was his destination.

"Joey, you and Jeb ride back home. If she touches into Welaka, get any news you can about Jacksonville, and the Feds, You men," Winston pointed to a a cluster of less agile troopers in a hodgepodge of uniform and homespun clothing, "remain here until we get back. Clean it up a bit, eh?"

He couched his command in a taunt, sweeping his eyes over the space they occupied atop the bluff.

"Be ready to move out by the time we get back."

While he talked he moved toward his own mount. His brother and others assigned scouting roles and sharp-shooters, readied their own steads.

"What's that?" Swep cocked his head, straining to isolate a sound above the bustle about him.

All movement ceased about him, spreading through the camp to the hushing of others. Faintly the putt-putt-putt of *Juanita*'s familiar engine replaced the deeper, receding clunking of *St. Mary*'s paddles. The sound carried across the water and above tree-tops to their elevated site. Once again the noise changed pitch when the steam-launch altered course, idled for a minute or so, them resumed its up-river movement, getting still louder in its approach toward the troop.

"What's he up to?" Winston's expressed thought echoed the puzzled looks on faces looking at him.

"That's yo' pappa's Cuban, eh." The gob of chewed

tobacco spat onto flattened grass may have been just to clear the mess out of his mouth, or to reflect the trooper-neighbor's opinion of Winston's father-in-law's launch captain.

"Should be," Winston carefully replied. The depth of animosity to those who did not echo Southern sentiments was a powder-keg awaiting a spark to ignite it. "You boys keep an eye on her, too."

Joey and Jeb, the tow-haired cousins when boys easy to spot with their flaxen hair atop sun-burned faces, nodded their darken-haired heads in unison, with a grin to their old gang member. Winston was always the leader.

They wheeled their ponies south. Winston turned north and in moments camp Bison settled down to a scene of placid domesticity, tin-plates scoured with sugar-sand, bedding rolled and secured atop haversacks, cooking fire banked for later use and water canteens topped up.

Chapter 2

Allegiances

Carlos Sanchez thrust another log into *Juanita*'s ravenous mouth, kicked the cast-iron stove door closed, lay one hand gently on the throttle and hooked a foot over her tiller.

They had slipped into the northern branch of Dunn's Creek when the steamer and tow he followed during the night from Jacksonville, took a wide turn to port into the mainstream. Sanchez knew every creek, stream, river and sinkhole between the Jacksonville port city gateway to the Atlantic, and the tiny communities between it and beyond.

On the move again, he barely spared a glance at the scuttled schooner with the tips of her masts securely tied down to the boles of deep-rooted cypress trees on Rat Island. Only the most observant would notice the few inches of the schooner's bulwark rail above water, mostly concealed amongst surface vegetation lazily flowing on out from Lake Crescent on the ebbing tide.

"There's no way out to the ocean," he mused aloud."Maybe they go to Haw Creek and the coast. What's there? Could be, they go to the big fort in St. Augustine?"

His brindle bulldog's tail thumped the deck-board when she heard her master's voice. Her deep throated growl had rumbled when she heard the shouts of men, unseen by her, calling from ship to shore scuttling *America*. The caution to 'hush', damped her instinct to bark aloud like she had been trained if any stranger approached *Juanita*. Scars on her flank and a chewed cheek which caused her left eye to be permanently open gave the former fighting-dog a fearsome appearance. Not unlike her master whose gunpowder-blackened cheek bore testimony to a closely discharged pistol; just before the cutlass wielded by Carlos, hacked his opponent's hand off.

Folks up and down the river called him 'Bryant's pirate', whether they knew about his former activities with the brotherhood that plagued merchantmen plying the Caribbean islands until the early 1800's. Not all were caught. Not all were hung. Carlos, who had an aptitude for things mechanical, had run a steam launch from ship to shore in the Cuban harbor of Havana when *Senor* Bryant, on one of his many visits, had engaged him in conversation and later, employed him.

"Why did you bring that pirate home with you," Rebecca had scolded.

"If you want to fight a pirate – hire a pirate," Bryant shrugged. "I gave him land for his hacienda, his pigs, his mother and the family."

Rebecca's eyebrows raised.

"Yes, m'dear. Even pirates have mothers, sometimes wives and many times, children. His swashbuckling days are over. But his extended family will range from here to Jacksonville, and every stop between. Their loyalty, to me, is guaranteed," he rubbed thumb and fingers together. "And their *tio*, Uncle Carlos, eh?"

During the intervening years *Juanita*'s portly captain, scarred dog and regular calls with stores and mail, had become a familiar and welcome sight, to most folks. The tid-bits of gossip collected on his route; plus reports from his family of Bryant-hired shipping agents, kept a finger on the pulse of the communities. Often that information determined whether to import and ship favored items for redistribution, before competitors read about trends in newspapers and magazines. As a newsman himself, Bryant had ears and eyes strained in Florida and its business partners in Cuba, for information and trends.

This latest expedition, to follow the escaping tug-boat and its tow, determining its destination, then report back, smacked of a little adventure and change from routine for Carlos and *Juanita*.

~~~

Pre-war feelings, by large slave-holding investors in the newly-opened land of Eden who mostly hailed south of Pennsylvania and west of Delaware; the so-called Mason-Dixon line, ran hot for the south and at boiling-point for any opposition.

The sparsely populated population of Putnam County numbered less than 3,000 on the cusp of the conflict between the states. It had more than quadrupled since the end of the Seminole wars with the promise of free and homesteaded land.

A major investor along the eastern banks of the St. Johns River, near the county seat of Palatka, was a syndicate of three good old southern boys headed by a Dr. Ralph Mays. With a swath of land rich in timber, trees to tap for turpentine and a saw-mill to supply wood for building at home and further afield, plus cleared acreages of established citrus groves, it required almost a hundred slave laborers to operate it.

Dr. Mays was a big fish in the political pool of Putnam County. Anyone opposed to him, was an enemy.

The sympathies of the Yankee trader Bryant were well-known but tolerated before secession, due to the service his launch supplied with delivery of imported goods; and the status of US Mail carrier. *Juanita*'s one-lung engine, its faded canopy and the familiar rotund figure of Carlos Sanchez, were recognizable to all riverside dwellers. Mays and company had tried unsuccessfully, to turf the Cuban and his master's boat, off the river. He even wanted *Juanita* seized as a trophy of war and one of his cronies, a shipping agent based in Jacksonville, to take on the role.

"If it wasn't for Miss Rebecca, her daughter and son-in-law Colonel Stephens and his troop, I'd take 'em on meself," Dr. Mays would brag privately to intimates who dined at his colonnaded riverfront mansion on the eastern shore, a few miles north of the waterfront city.

His views were well-known in the area. He frequently appeared at meetings both official, run by city fathers, and others among fellow plantation owners. Topics ranged from the purely domestic; expanding tracks, paths and roads for general use. That included acquisition of rights of way sites for anticipated railroad expansion and setting permanent moorings to ferry goods between shore and ship while the main jetty into deep-water was occupied. There had even been talk of street-lighting with kerosene-lamps, before secession arrived and skilled workers departed.

He too had heard the rumble of St. *Mary*'s paddle-wheels churning across the wide westward expanse of the river, more like a lake, before she followed the sharp bend south to Palatka. Comfortable under the eiderdown, imported from Europe years earlier, he could picture the vessel and wondered if it bore news from the front.

Even if he had been awake he would not have seen her tow, made familiar to all his proud countrymen from woodcuts, newspapers, magazines and calendars which displayed the distinctive raked masts and sharp bowsprit of the schooner *America*. Mist shrouded her from observers ashore, apart from a few pre-dawn fishermen angling for food to feed the plantation slaves.

Shortly after the clunk-clunk-clunk of *Juanita*'s easily recognizable engine, wafted ashore.

Dr. May only learned later, during routine conversations with his majordomo, of the fisherman's sighting of a sleek sailing ship under tow. During the following days, with renewed activities on the river and the first appearance of a Union gunboat, he connected the pieces together.

The picture created sent the doctor's heart racing and

his bile rising triggering a series of decisions which would culminate in a disastrous, and deadly, reaction.

~~~

An accurately aimed precious stub of white chalk left its mark on the shaved black head of argumentative Bobby Davis, nipping his next comment before he could utter it.

"Ouch!"

"Now, bring that back to me, after you 'pologise to massa Harold there for what you jus' said." Burrel's deep voice quieted the chatter of speculation which interrupted the class reading session. The small room, off the main body of the structure slaves built for religious services, served both Bible-study and schooling since the proper school's teacher left to enlist.

"He called me a nigger, Mister Burrel," Bobby protested. He rubbed his head, found on the floor the missile which had stung him, and turned toward the school-master.

"A-pol-o-gise," Burrel enunciated.

"I'se sorry ah called you perckerwood...but yo' called me a nigger, furst," Bobby rushed.

The class laughed. A frown creased Burrel's forehead. His eyes shifted from the approaching boy and the red-faced homesteader's son, mouth agape, sitting on the bench clutching the slate on his knees, to the frayed switch atop his desk-podium.

The eyes of every student followed his. Silence descended after a brief flutter of speculative whisperings, under Burrel's glare.

Bobby's steps faltered.

He too looked at the switch.

"Massa Davis. You gotta respect and make allowances for the slow of learning. You knows how to treat yo' elders and betters, ain't that so?"

Bobby nodded. Harold smirked.

"Well now. We all knows things at different times. You jus' happen to pick up the rhythm of the words and the letters of the alphabet, easy. For some," Burrel's eyes swept along the bench, to the shuffling of feet; some bare, others shod, on the gray pine-boards, "it takes a bit longer. Now, we all know who's good at sums – and..."

His remark drowned under the titter of children ranging from barely five years old, to a couple of boys with stubble in their chins.

Harold was a natural with figures and could add, subtract and multiply in his head before others could render the answer on their slates. But, his fingers failed to translate into figures and letters, as easily. That was where the competitive play-yard and fishing friends parted ways. Bobby's figures and block letters were text-book perfect.

"Now some of us, we learned early, how to address each other, right class?"

"Yes sir, Mister Burrel, sir," chorused his pupils.

"So, you learned early from the Colonel, yo' momma and me, how you talk to people according to their rank, age and occupation, in the house, the field and the home of the Lord. Ain't that so."

"Yes sir, Mister Burrel, sir."

"Now, some of us forgits; jus' like we don't remember our figures and letters, all the time. But, we gotta make that effort. ALL the time." His voice deepened and arose, just as it did when he reached the conclusion of a sermon.

"We don't carry that playground and backwoods talk into the classroom. Do we?"

"No sir, Mister Burrel, sir."

Harold joined in the chorus, catching the eye of Bobby who grinned back, before glancing at the switch.

Burrel did not miss a thing. His hand reached for the switch, clasped it and gave a practice swish through the air before it smacked loudly atop the empty desk. Its thwack echoed loudly, causing many squints and clenched teeth in the classroom.

"Do you think we've learned anything, today?" His

glance darted between the two wide-eyed boys and staring children.

"YES, SIR."

"Right. Go back to your seat. And praise the Lord you can sit down, without pain – this time."

A ripple of laughter and a few good-nature slaps and tugs followed Bobby back to his place.

"Now. Who's gonna be first to read from the blackboard…" The switch in his hand pointed to a somewhat wavy-lined rendering of The Lord's Prayer.

Hands shot into the air.

"…from here," the switch descended on a word two-thirds down." Hands fell down like trees in a hurricane. Most knew the prayer by rote. Few were able to take on the task. Bobby's hand stood high, waving, but he had played his role for the day.

"Miss Sally. Let's hear from you."

A shy child in a worn blue-gingham dress, carefully adjusted from an older sister, gripped her slate and got to her feet."

"Forgive us our trespasses as we forgive those who trespass against us," she began.

Burrel nodded while observing the exchange of glances between pupils in a cross-section of the community, representing the next generation of Welaka citizens. If they survived the conflict ahead.

Chapter 3

Preparing

Outriders from Winston's troop reached Rose Cottage with news of the scuttling and possibilities of Federal action to follow while field hands were digging the ditch from Acosta Creek to the new gin-mill site.

Octavia and her mother were scouring the ledgers at Rose Cottage containing goods sold, debts owed, wages paid and profits made, when the halloo of the exuberant boy-men sent chickens scampering and dogs barking.

"What now?" Rebecca's face was already scrunched up from the taste of substitute coffee.

It was made from burned cottonseed blended with a soupcon of real coffee. Apart from its taste, an improvement over potato, rye or grits ersatz blends, was its purported additional prowess. Some claimed it was less harmful to persons of a nervous disposition. In Rebecca's case that supposed gain was subverted by the irritant of having to swallow the mixed solution: "because of the damn Yankee blockade".

They both crossed to the window, then bustled to the kitchen door where the riders watered their horses, and themselves from a bucket and ladle Mama Burrel offered them.

"What do you mean: 'The Yankees are coming'?" Rebecca demanded.

The cavalrymen, who may have presented fearful foes to any blue-coats facing them, were still just neighbor boys playing soldiers, to the Bryant matriach.

"The colonel sez y'all should pack up provisions and take to the woods, ma'am," the older one with corporal chevrons on his sleeve, tugged the peak of his kepi with a respectful salute. "There's something going on up Dunn's Creek way. A big schooner boat's been sunk there. And the *St. Mary*'s took off into the lake."

His outreached arm pointed south-east in the general direction of Lake Crescent.

"Yeah. The colonel reckons the Feds won't be far behind." The younger soldier blurted out."

"We gotta go, ma'am. Warn the rest of the folks. Much obliged for the water."

Both women stepped back to avoid the panting steeds who where whirled about to set out along the wagon-rutted route to Welaka.

The dinner-bell calling field-hands and all others within hearing to attend Rose Cottage, sounded out under the firm hand of the cook even before Rebecca and Octavia discussed their next move.

Rebecca's eyes glinted for a moment before her daughter steered her away from a territorial squabble.

"Momma, we've got to load up all hands, and move, now. We can discuss the future, when we're safely hidden," Octavia insisted.

Burrel, field-hands, ditch-diggers, children and their mothers began gathering around Rose Cottage. Some wept, others cried excitedly, but all eyes were on the acknowledged leader, though not the owner, of the holdings in the absence of the colonel.

The women, white and black, swept through the kitchen selecting cooking utensils, tin plates, mugs, buckets and all manner of items they would need. Eager hands reached to carry or pack into sacks, barrels or tubs.

A housemaid created bundles of bedding and pillows and sent for tarpaulins and canvas to create shelters.

A crocodile of helpers followed Burrel and Rebecca to the storage cave to load wheelbarrows and the service wagon.

"We'd best leave the horses here. Their neighing could give us away," Burrel advised.

"How..."

"Those boys are strong as horses, ain't ya?" he challenged striplings who flexed arms, grinning widely. "We'll hitch 'em up. Let's get to it," his explanation and reaction to Octavia's poised question rolled into one.

She darted a glance of gratitude to Burrel before returning to Rose Cottage.

"Girls," she called out to a kitchen-maid and washer-woman to follow her. They stopped by the warehouse where bales of cotton were stockpiled, along with indigo vials and bricks of resin awaiting shipment if and when the blockade lifted.

The powers that be in the Confederate strategy team with the ear of Jefferson Davis, calculated the ruckus caused by lack of raw material reaching England from its northern mills would force the British government to side with the south. It took a while for the south to realize the industrialized European centers could profit more from war than a peaceful, competing, rival.

The resin blocks, tapped from the same pine trees which produced turpentine after distillation, were destined for European fiddlers.

"Emma, put these in the double-pot and gently stir it. You don't want to set a fire and singe away your hair now, do you?"

The young girl with locks of braided hair no bandana could contain flashed a wide toothy smile.

"No ma'am."

Octavia no longer noticed the transition of address from Miss to Ma'am which accompanied her passage from a single carefree girl, to a wife and mother of one toddler and possibly, another on the way.

The sturdy broad-beamed, hard-of-hearing washerwoman who merely grunted responses, stood waiting. Her arms switched from hanging by her sides to folding over her ample belly and pendulous bosoms.

Octavia beckoned, leading the way to the dining room and the sideboard containing flatware and silver. She opened the drawers to lay the contents atop the green baize which protected its polished surface. From another drawer she pulled and stacked precious linen napkins and tablecloths trimmed with lace and intricate needlework patterns.

Carefully she took a silver fork, took one roll of a napkin, placed another next to it, and rolled again before adding more to demonstrate how the cutlery should be bundled. She held up both hands, fingers spread, indicating how many minutes before she returned, then swept out toward her bedroom. The covers, sheets, pillow and comforter were already stripped and aboard the wagon. The adjustable three-mirror dressing-table, a wedding gift from her parents, stood beckoning from the soft light from the north window.

A sigh escaped, taking the domestic scene in, perhaps for the last time, before crossing purposefully to the trinket box, and the hidden drawer containing the seldom-worn valuable dress-jewelry. Some she had selected herself in Boston, other pieces came from family heirlooms. A velvet purple scarf more decorative than practical, substituted for napkins to protectively roll the precious items into a priceless trove. She slipped the parcel of items into a suede bag, secured it with a leather thong, automatically glanced at her reflected selves, tucked a wisp of hair in place.

She fetched a flannel pillowcase from the cedar linen-box at the foot of the canopied double-bed then returned to the dining room. Several tightly-rolled bundles occupied the table surface. The girl stood, dry-washing her hands anxiously watching Octavia.

"That's wonderful." A smile and nod of the head stemmed the agitated hand-rubbing and brought a grimace in return.

"Now..." The pillowcase was opened, put in the girl's hands while Octavia carefully loaded it. A stout belt bound around its knotted opening, secured its contents and formed a loop which would soon show its full potential.

Back in the kitchen the pungent smells wrinkled her nose but she smiled approvingly after a glance at the liquified amber resin surrounded by bubbling water.

"Good." The girl's braids shook from her nodded response.

Sounds of activity from the nearby yard, pens and cages where livestock grunted and squawked at the interruption to its daily routine and transfer into a Noah's Ark parade of animals being marched off into the wilderness, reminded them, time was precious.

"Quick, but careful, remove the boiler from the heat. We need—aha—this will work." Octavia selected a three-legged iron pot to place on the chopping block.

"Pour about a third in it..."

The toffee-like liquid was transferred. Then, with a final kiss, Octavia placed the jewel-packed bag atop the fast-setting resin.

"Slowly, add the rest. Here," she reached forward to aid the girl, using a swab of damp scrubbing rags to take the weight and tilt the pot.

The liquid stopped an inch shy of the rim. They all peered at the contents rapidly solidifying with the pale outline of its valuable contents suspended and protected from the elements.

"Don't let anyone near it." Octavia admonished before steering the washer-woman away from Rose Cottage to the site of the secluded privy reserved for immediate family.

During the next hour while occupants of the Rose Cottage community relocated furnishing and supplies to a make-shift home of refuge, Octavia and her helpers concealed the waterproof packages of family silver in the most odoriferous of locations to deter detection. They then submerged the weighted resin-bound valuables contained in the cast-iron pot, to the depths of the newly-created gin-still pond.

Chapter 4

Search

A pall of smoke sat over the smoldering city of Jacksonville, mingling with the last wisps of sea mist which clung to the shoreline on either side of *Ottawa*'s cautious approach.

She had pulled ahead of the main body of vessels concentrated near Fort Steele which had been abandoned before they landed the first marine ashore. Guns were still mounted on carriages, loaded and primed to discharge. Ammunition was in plentiful supply, as were the commissary larders and gated fruit and vegetable bins. No dogs remained, but the eyes of feral cats peered from the shadow of abandoned wagons and between barrels of water stored in anticipation of a siege.

Florida was abandoned for the first time in the conflict which pitted families against each other, in a strategic withdrawal – by both sides – to wage war elsewhere.

A few shots fired from militia muskets ashore, which fell far short of the gunboat, did not merit firing her swivel bow-gun, the Dahlgren smooth-bore capable of hurling an 11-inch shell into the sparely defended countryside. Ahead, the stark black beams of a community in ruins poked above the ground-mist, concealing unknown dangers.

The helmsman's eyes followed Sam's hand-signals given from his perch from the bare-pole of the forward mast, while *Ottawa*'s engine steadily vibrated underfoot, slowly pushing her nose through the ebbing waters. She wound her way through the curves of sandy shores ringed with the natural and man-made detritus which attracted winged, clawed and two-legged beachcomber hunters.

Eventually, without a shot of subsequence being fired at her, she made her way into Jacksonville toward the longest remaining pier where a huddle of people, beneath a white-sheet flying from an improvised flag-pole, awaited them.

Less than a hundred feet from land, she hove to. Her broadside guns had the group in its sights. Crews at the bow and stern guns stood ready and focused, and marksmen manning her side stood with cocked weapons ready.

"Lt. Vincent, take a crew to the delegation and bring back no more than three representatives from the city to parley. Despite the destruction, the inhabitants appear welcoming," Lt. Stevens lowered his telescope. "Lt. Taylor, stand by with the boarding party to explore ashore, as soon as we ascertain their intentions."

Sam, eager to step on dry-land after weeks of sea-duty, and curious to confirm his eyes had not deceived him in sighting the yacht *America,* dreaded what he might find in the destroyed docks and boatyard westward from their location. He acknowledged the order and joined the 'knuckle squad', as the first wave of boarders were known. For good reason.

At first the boarders resented the scrawny Jerseyite's leadership until, during a fisticuffs drill based on the sport of boxing, the agile lieutenant landed a blow to the plexus followed by a one-two knock-out combination which felled their champion.

"But that's not fair, sir," the mess-deck lawyer within the group, spluttered.

"Fair, Murphy, fair? We fight to win. Not to please a boxing judge." Sam snarled in a rare display of anger. He forced himself to take a deep breath to control the timbre of his voice."I can assure you, from personal experience, Sandy Hook hearties do not play by the Marquis of Queensbury Rules when someone spills grog on 'em in a bar-fight."

While Murphy skulked at the put down, his mates drowned his protest with a cheer and laughter which acknowledged the 'whorefiscer', as they disparagingly referred to those who ruled the quarter-deck, was one of them.

Sambuca's instinct drove him to join the waiting men, weaving his way between legs and outreaching arms until he reached Sam's side.

Absently chewing on a piece of hard-tack he'd tucked into a waistcoat pocket, Sam scratched the feline's head.

"Tommy.," He called to a ship's powder-boy idling on an upturned bucket by the gun-crew.

"Sir."

"Take Sambuca to the galley." The cat's ears twitched. "Then put him in the c-a-g-e,"he spelled out the word,"and stow him in my quarters until we get back."

The squad smirked. Sambuca's suspicions were aroused, but he recognized the word galley and sensed there would be a tit-bit waiting when the boy set him down. They turned their attention to some sort of commotion riling the group gathered at the end of the pier. All envied the cat's hearing abilities.

But Sam's ears caught just one word drifting across the water.

America

~ ~ ~

James Bryant ears perked up when the representative from the Union gunboat identified himself, and named *Ottawa*'s captain.

"Did you say Holdup Stevens?" His voice cut through the babble of platitudes from the mayor, the sheriff and other politicos gathered to greet the Yankee sailors.

"Aye." Vincent's eyes swiveled from the pudgy faced platitudes of the mayor and growling countenance of the sheriff; who had twice referred to 'damnyankees' in offering no resistance to them stepping ashore.

"My family is close to his. Is he the Commodore's son?"

Bryant asked.

"Lieutenant Steven's Jr., is the late Commodore's son, aye."

"Then please convey me to him, immediately," Bryant ignored the hostile glances of some in the delegation who were less than desirous of entertaining the Union ships, or crew. "I have information of vital use which I cannot reveal, before the present company."

The urgency in his voice, the educated northern vowels and earnestness of his presentation, plus the claim to family connections, convinced the liaison officer to include Bryant with the mayor and Sheriff.

Bryant's was the one familiar face of the burghers of the southern city to step onto *Ottawa*'s deck, the captain recognized when the delegation boarded the gunboat.

Protocol demanded the officials be greeted first, but they were swiftly shown below to the captain's quarters while the two men warmly shook hands and exchanged news of friends and family up north before Bryant made his purpose known.

Despite their lowered voices, once again Sam's acute hearing picked out the word *America*, carried upon the sea-breeze. It was no surprise, therefore, when he was summoned and instructed to listen to Bryant's tale, while the captain rejoined the city fathers.

~~~

"What you see before you is an act of wanton vandalism," Bryant swept his arm across the smoldering city landscape. "What they could not carry away with them, they destroyed. Most will not realize, until they run shy of a few meals and goods which make life tenable in this wilderness state, they have shot themselves in the foot. Their act has crippled the state for a decade, or more."

Sam nodded sympathetically to the shaking gray-haired gentleman's bitter comments.

"And the schooner?" He prompted.

"Ah yes." Bryant smiled wryly. "The prize, eh?"

"I have a deeper interest in her than prize-money, sir." Sammy allowed a little scorn to creep into his voice. "As a boy, she was my home when I had none. She is directly responsible for these." His fingers clasped the two gold-braid rings on his blue-uniform jacket.

Bryant's eyebrows rose.

"I certainly meant no disrespect, young man. I had no idea of your close connection. This is most fortuitous, for you will be familiar with her basic measurements; overall length, breadth and depth. I hope she has merely been hidden from sight in a creek, or scuttled, and pray she has not been set afire." Once again, Bryant's hand encompassed the scene ashore.

Sam's rigid shoulders relaxed slightly at the conciliatory tone of the Floridian. His connections with the captain, his knowledge of the local population and its terrain; plus a vested interest in returning to a business state of *status quo*, could prove invaluable. He glanced at the shore crew cooling its heels, not too quietly, shooting occasional glances his way.

"Perhaps you'd care to join us, sir?"

"What?"

"We are going ashore to assess the damage, its resources for occupation and potential for a coaling-base," he explained.

Bryant pursed his lips, pondering momentarily before nodding acquiescence. His glance at the toughs forming the landing party, and the casual but familiar way they handled their weapons, encouraged his decision.

"I sent my man aboard the steam-launch *Juanita* to follow *America's* wake," he said. "He should be returning soon with news, unless some evil has befallen him. In the meantime, there are families; refugees from the mob, hidden on the west-bank."

His voice trailed off at the emergence of the mayor,

sheriff and captain onto the main-deck. The civilians glance toward him. Bryant made no move to join them when they were ushered to the boarding steps to gingerly clamber aboard the waiting pinnace, under the watchful eye of a senior midshipman who would set them ashore.

The captain beckoned.

"Mr. Bryant, perhaps you'd care to join me for a late breakfast?" He offered. A nod to Sam dismissed him to his previous task."

"Sir, we need..."

"We need to await the rest of the squadron to join us and take up station to secure the community," Stevens rode over him "An independent assessment of the situation ashore is eagerly awaited, Mister Taylor, before any further expeditions can be mounted. Is that clear?

"Aye, aye, sir." Despite his anxiety to seek out and save *America,* Sam realized the tenuous position the sole Union ship held in the heart of Dixie. He saluted, nodded his head to Bryant, and set off ashore.

Part VI

Expedition

Chapter 1

Expedition

A cluster of buildings ahead of *Ottawa's* starboard bow, where the broad St. Johns River narrowed to a few hundred feet between its banks, denoted Palatka's presence. It was the terminal site for most commercial river traffic.

The wharves were quiet. Moorings empty. Jetties bare of any vessels save one flying the Union flag.

But the shore was lined with people, some waving, some stern-faced and anxious at the sight of a Federal gunboat. Its 11-inch Dahlgren swivel gun pointed toward their community, her decks were manned by armed marines and sailors and two cannons run out from her sides ready to fire.

"Ah, there she is." Bryant called out and pointed toward the distinctive hull, funnel and canopy of his steam launch *Juanita.*

"We'll get to that." Stevens snapped.

It was a tense moment. His ship was fast approaching a population whom within the next few minutes would prove their hospitality, or hostility. He was in unknown territory both figuratively and literally. None aboard *Ottawa* knew the natives or territory save the Connecticut merchantman who could be playing his own game, at odds to Federal interests.

The Florida state flag was the only one flying ashore. The state was the third to join the secessionists, February, 1861. It had done so by unanimous vote by Tallahassee legislators in the state capitol. Stevens was well aware of the separatist fervor and tactics of intimidation, up to arson and including murder to persuade any overt opposition.

Palatka's real or apparent role would determine its future within the next hour or so.

~~~

Juanita tied up to the gunship's port entrance, was concealed from sight of Palatka's citizens.

Not so from Dr. Mays and his partners, who viewed all the activity from the far shore to the east in the comfort of padded open coaches. They were serviced by liveried coachmen and house-servants who had followed in a dray loaded with drinks and refreshments.

There was a festive air amongst the ladies and children who accompanied the planters party. It was not reflected in the tirade of abuse hurled toward the Yankee visitors, and specifically at Welaka's founder James Bryant and his launch-captain Carlos Sanchez.

"Sonsabitches have sold us out." Mays hollered out to his partners and all within hearing.

However, his fellow southern speculators were less distraught than he. They focused not so much on the speculative land-grab in Florida, than the inherited interests of their old southern home-front where opposing armies were gathering strength for another battle. They feared it would not be a rout against Yankee aggression, like the first clash. While the south's rural soldiers were raised with the familiarity of firing weapons on an almost daily basis, pitted against a citizenry of pen-pushers raised in street-lit cities, their northern brethren had Yankees learned a costly lesson from the Bull Run debacle

The doctor's telescope followed every movement of the hotly gesticulating Cuban talking with his boss and a young blue-uniformed officer who joined them aboard the steam launch. After a few minutes the officer clambered onto the gunboat, disappeared below then re-appeared with a group of armed men who followed him aboard *Juanita*. Once settled, lines were cast off and the little steam launch chugged away with the inflowing tide south before the bend of Devil's Elbow concealed them.

"What are they up to?" Mays posed the question.

No one responded.

~~~

The rumble of her engines alerted wildlife along the shores which set off the birds which roused the dogs and caused shore-dwellers to glance toward the river. A ribbon of black coal-smoke dispersed in *Ottawa*'s wake, thick and oily, its soot settling on the uttermost leaves and branches of tall cypress trees centuries old.

Bowmen scoured the water ahead for submerged waterlogged trunks, ready to fend them off with boarding-pikes to protect her hull, the single-screw and the unmanned bobbing *Juanita* on a short tow-line, weaving from side to side. The ship barely had steerage way against the ebbing current while she cautiously wound her way upstream toward Dunn's Creek.

Sanchez glanced back at *Juanita* where the river widened, except for a wooded island west whose tree-limbs were black with buzzards carefully watching a potential meal passing by. He stood close to the helmsman, occasionally ordering a wheel adjustment to keep them in deeper water. The Captain and Bryant stood on the port side of the bridge where a light sea-breeze wafted across the Florida peninsular to fill the steadying sail. Sam made rough sketches and notes in his journal from the vantage point of height and a steady platform.

Hours earlier *Juanita*'s wallowing progress with an overload of armed men scouring the vistas which unfolded beyond every bend, left little time to do more than observe and make mental notes. Now, on his second trip, he even recognized odd tree-clumps, an oyster-shell mound from antiquity and fallen logs flattened in the path of a hurricane-spawned tornado.

"Not much further, eh?"

"*Si, senor.*"

"Ten to fifteen minutes," Sam called to the captain.

"It's likely the local militia will have prepared a reception for us," Bryant cautioned. "Regretfully, my son-in-law Winston – also a Stephens with a 'ph' – may be there too. His cavalry troop patrols this area."

"Hmnn. We'll be prepared. But they are not our first priority. Raising *America* is. Taylor, you say she was above water, but submerged."

"Her stern rail showed, at low-tide, sir." Sam responded. "The tips of her masts could be seen secured to trees ashore. Our pilot claims she sits in about three-fathoms overall, but the creek bottom could have shoaled from erosion or tide action. There's still the steamer..."

"Later, Taylor, later. *America* is the prize. The sooner we get her up the better for her, and us." Stevens snapped. His eyes darted from shore to shore, anticipating a sharp-shooter at any moment. He consoled himself his uniform was not as flamboyant as the Confederates whose wide gold-braid chevrons denoting rank emblazoned on their sleeves were an irresistible sniper target. Cartoons by some wags, which appeared in the new illustrated magazines, showed legions of Johnny Reb officers with their arms in slings. He had no desire to join them.

Several gaps in the seaward shoreline heralded their approach to a wider stream flowing on the north shore of Rat Island, whose southern edge marked the entrance to Dunn's Creek and the scuttled ship.

"Bo'sun, stand by. Engine-room, standby"

Sam's call, alerting the anchor-crew and his call through the voice-pipe to warn the chief-engineer of imminent activity, raised the level of awareness aboard the gunboat.

The appearance of her bow-wave entering Dunn's Creek was observed by many hidden eyes beyond the shrubs, creepers and ferns rimming Murphy Island's north shore, where Winston's troop lay in wait.

Sam was glad he still had his winter-gear unpacked, despite the warnings of northern friends who had joshed him about melting away under the hot Florida sun. On that mid-March morning he again saw *America* for the first time in more than a decade, a thin layer of ice had formed on the water cask, and the iron-rails atop *Ottawa*'s bridge were frigid to the touch. He felt no qualms about wearing navy-blue wool mittens while on watch.

When he and Sanchez first entered Dunn's Creek the previous day the triangular shape of *America*'s starboard-quarter stern rail poked above the placid surface.

It triggered a flood of bitter-sweet memories. He had clung desperately to that rail while Atlantic waves slapped and rolled under her tossing hull on his knees hurling his dinner over the side to the amusement of the crew. Even when he gained his sea-legs a few days later, he felt the shame every time he passed that spot. While he could laugh about that ancient incident. he still recalled the taste of bile rising from his gut.

"That's her stern rail, starboard side," he explained to Sanchez. "Let's circle her, take a few soundings and set a team on shore where the masts are secured." His remarks were heard by his men, and Winston's concealed troop peering down the barrels of loaded but un-cocked muskets.

Jaunita's engine sat silent while Sanchez sculled her with a large oar slotted in a groove in her transom. The wildlife fell silent in the immediate area, while further afield birds and squirrels chattered in the trees. There was no movement of *America*'s exposed rail, indicating she was solid on the creek bed and impervious to the tug of the tide. Stout lines held her lower masts secure ashore, barely breaking the surface just before the edge of Rat Island. No spars or sails could be seen. The murky brownish water made viewing her hull from the surface difficult. Sam managed to make out dark patches where hatch-covers were opened to the elements.

He waded ashore into the undergrowth which had been hacked clear into pathways leading to the anchor points. A yelp and loud splash heralded a piglet-sized water-rat escaping the jet of urine directed into the creek by a startled crewman.

"Now you know why its called Rat Island," the boson called out. "Quit yer lollygagging. Could be a snake takes a bite outta your pride and joy next time, eh?"

The incident eased the tension but alerted *Ottawa*'s crew there were more things to be wary of than suspected rebels, behind every shrub.

Neatly-coiled lines lay next to the base of tree-trunks securing *America*'s masts. The lines ran slack, draped over bushes bent down under their weight.

"Detach those lines, while we can, She might shift to an even keel and bring her rigging above water,"Sam instructed.

The mast-top tangle of knots were unraveled and the line draped over shoulders to make for easier transport back to the creek-edge. Sam noted several other stout trees which might be useful as anchors to maneuver the submerged hull. Within the hour Dunn's Creek was silent again except for the fading thumping of *Juanita*'s engine fading in the distance, and raised voices from Murphy Island.

"We could have taken 'em." Winston's younger brother echoed the sentiments of many of the troop who silently glowered at their leader.

"And brought the wrath of Union troops to plunder, pillage and rape like we heard they did in Fernandina?" Winston answered the question with a question."They're not aware, or interested in us or our families, yet. They just want their prize. Let 'em have it. It's no use to you is it – Captain Bligh?"

His jibing tone raised a few smiles, easing the hostility of the young bloods but bolstering the empathy of family-men who had concerns greater than winging a few Yankees. All were familiar with the epic sea-yarn of the British ship *Bounty,* her mutinous crew and eventual fate. It also carried a reminder to familiar neighbors and family; there were consequences for disobeying military orders, no matter how close and casual the unit was.

Rumors of Union outrages aided by freed slaves, swept through southern states ahead of the arrival of federal troops and sailors. They were fed by fears of carnage similar to that which occurred in the French islands of the Caribbean. Only the volume of bragging by mostly untested Confederate volunteers drowned out the dire warnings.

"They'll be back. And as long as we don't stir them up like a nest of hornets, will go about their business and stay clear of our homes. If, when it come to it, we will face them down. But not until *they* fire the first shot," Winston raised his voice so all would hear. "Now, brother, use some of your energy to spread the word to take to the woods for a few days while we assess the situation."

Swep scowled but mounted up.

"Looks like we'll be here for a while, lads. Let's set up camp beyond the rise, south, select some observation sites and breastworks from logs while we can, in case we need 'em." Winston's call for action relieved any doubts he was ready to make a run for safety. He was setting up to make a stand, if necessary.

Chapter 2

Refugees

Swep's arrival on a lathered horse shouting warnings of "enemy in sight" stirred up the nervous families who had gravitated back to their familiar routines, more out of boredom than defiance.

"Damned fool boy," Rebecca railed when he dismounted in a cloud of dust, grinning from ear to ear. "Look what you've done. Panicked them. They're running 'round like chickens without a head."

His spontaneous prank shattered the bucolic atmosphere surrounding 'Rose Cottage' sparking the underlying fears and panic held in check by the stoic guidance of Rebecca and Octavia. Swep realized it may not have been the smartest stunt to pull.

"Ah'm truly sorry Miss Rebecca, ma'am. And you too, Tivie." He stepped away from his sister-in-law who was swiping at him with a twig-broom. "But the bluecoats are here. Or were," he added.

"Burrel. Git over here, listen to what he says," the matriarch called out. The foreman, preacher, hunter and slave who all deferred to in the absence of any white overseers, lumbered up to them.

Swep glanced at the familiar face of the man who had taught him fun stuff like fishing and snaring rabbits; plus practical tasks like sharpening tools and knives without lopping off a finger, and stripping and splitting logs for fences to corral livestock. They nodded, flushed under Burrel's cool stare.

"The Yankees were there. Up to Dunn's Creek, snooping around that schooner. We coulda took 'em too," Swep grinned. "But Winnie wouldn't let us."

"Thank the Lord there's someone with an ounce of sense between their ears," Rebecca scolded. "What does he want us to do?"

A goodly crowd gathered within earshot of Rose Cottage.

Burrel beckoned them closer.

"Let'em hear it from the horse's...mouth." Burrel paused just enough for his opinion of Swep's caper to register.

Both women smiled. Swep barely refrained from sticking his tongue out. "Won't hafta repeat it, Miz Rebecca."

"*Juanita*, cap'n Sanchez and the bluecoats rummaged around some, then took off down river. Winnie – the Colonel," Swep corrected himself under Rebecca's glance, "sez we're to dig in 'cos they'll be back. He told me to tell y'all and everyone I find, to keep the noise down, only light fires when the smoke blows away from the river, and stay away from it."

He counted the points on his fingers.

"If they don't know we're here, they won't be coming a lookin' for us. They jus' wants that boat"

"What's so special about it?" Tivie asked.

"Colonel says she's a Yankee racer who beat the Limey's back when he was a boy."

"The *America*?" Frowns wrinkled Rebecca's forehead. "Here?"

Her childhood in the seaport of Boston had ingrained

an empathy with its ships and sailors. Even after she married and moved north and south depending on the mercantile tides of fortune at the ports of Savannah and Jacksonville, sea stories kept her interest alive. Admittedly, back then she was more interested in the fashionable styles of Queen Victoria's England, when broadsheet accounts of the Great Exhibition were displayed. But those stories of *America's* valiant challenge and stunning victory had filled her with pride, at the time.

"What is it, Momma?" Tivie asked.

"Later child, later. Burrel, we must abandon our homes for the while and stay out of sight. "She emphasized the term. "And do as the Colonel says if we are to survive." She turned. "Quickly now Swepson, be on your way. And," she wagged a cautioning finger at him, "less drama"!

"And do not forget to pick up any mail from those folks," Tivie added. "Some haven't seen their menfolk for weeks. I'll have something for the Colonel, too."

Swep rolled his eyes, grinning when he shied away from the mock swipe of the broom Tivie raised.

"Here." Burrel reached into a burlap sack to scoop a handful of raisins, sun-dried from the grapevines out of Rosemary Cottage vegetable garden. Swep stuffed them into his overcoat pocket, smiling again. All was right with the world. And he had something sweet and nourishing to munch on during his rounds.

"Let us pray for his safety," Burrel implored those gathered about, "then get to work. For...?"

"The Lord will find mischief for idle hands," chorused the children in the group.

"Amen." Others, including Rebecca and Tivie, responded.

~~~

While Rebecca hustled the help and hindrances, created by mothers with children scurrying underfoot or wailing from makeshift cloth hip-slings, Tivie sought the sanctuary of her bedroom and a tiny desk to respond to Winston's latest letter.

The primitive messaging and mail service the riverside community had created was their only lifeline, despite their close proximity to each other. Troopers in the St. Johns Rangers could not leave their station overlooking the river. Especially Winston. The married men were concerned for their families, so near and far away. And the younger recruits missed their girlfriends, and mothers; though few would admit it.

Proper ink had been exhausted long ago, along with many other necessities since the blockade embargo of goods began. Crushed charcoal and burnt cork in water had been tried. The blotch product met with varying degrees of success. Some precious blocks of indigo, stockpiled along with bales of cotton in a Confederate ruse to tighten the raw-material market for English manufacturers to bring pressure on the government to win support for the southern cause, was broached. The purple penmanship was even more shocking to the reader when the same letter-paper, also in short supply, was used for a second time.

Tivie's dainty words, from top to bottom, crossed over Winston's heavier penmanship from side to side. It took good light and concentration to interpret their criss-cross correspondence.

"My own dear husband," she began. For the next few minutes she was transported from the chaos of preparing to seek refuge, hiding like fugitives from invasion. She filled the

space with home news of peach rows being planted by her younger brothers, of their first daughter Rosa splurting out how she missed her daddy. *"She said 'de papa don' for 'my dear Pa Pa gone' to herself while playing alone."*

Rosalie was the light in Winston's life. Tivie could imagine the misty-eyed look he would have when he read that.

Her news spoke of trees being felled and rolled for fuel and to make way for the plow to turn newly claimed growing-land, after Burrel burned off the brush. The encounter her mare Clara had with a branch which pierced her foreleg in a nasty gash. *"Burrel put tar and grease on it immediately and she appears to be recovering."* And then there was her brother's favorite boyhood companion, his dog Taylor, who began howling just as she concluded her letter. *"A tree came down on Henry's dog Taylor but we got him out and he seems to be recovering. Hopefully he will join our odyssey into the backwoods and survive, with us."*

She signed it*: As ever, Yr loving Wife* then folded it to conceal the contents and addressed it to Winston.

The world of reality intruded upon her brief escape with the sound of raised voices from the outside kitchen. The cook's shrill voice was unmistakable, as was the cracking voice of her youngest brother, thirteen year old George. A weak beam of sunlight framed her face for a moment, reflected in the dresser mirror. It showed lines of worry where laughter lines previously existed. With a sigh she turned toward the commotion to handle the latest household crisis.

~~~

Children swaddled in layers of clothing piled atop bundles of bedding, laughed with glee as the rolling wagon swayed along the rutted trail eastward to the line of trees which would become their temporary home. Older folks, perched with them were upset at the changing scenery, the noisy clattering of wagon-wheels which jostled pots and pans strung along the wagon's sides, and the crack of the driver's whip urging yoked oxen forward.

Rebecca and Tivie watched from a knoll, topped by a massive spreading live oak which gave cattle shady relief during scorching summer-months, in the comfort of the Sunday buggy for church services and social visits.

The exodus from Rose Cottage, more than the perpetual shortages which had reduced them to sharecropper diets and yesteryear fashions, the loss of white manpower from preachers to schoolmaster, husbands and sons due to the war beyond the horizon, brought the war into focus.

Rebecca held the reins while Burrel led his people and Tivie cradled Rosa, sucking her thumb in slumber, against the prominent mound of her next child.

"I so wish this stupid war was over and we were left in peace to live our lives as the Lord intended," she cried.

"Girl. That's what we are fighting for. To take back what is rightfully ours, without outside interference," Rebecca shot back. "These man-made laws go against the Word. It is written, in the holy book: 'Slaves, obey your earthly masters with fear and trembling.' "She quoted Ephesians 6:5 by rote.

Spittle lined her pursed lips.

With a sharp jerk of her hands she slapped the horse's rump to urge it forward, guiding it with a firm tug toward procession.

Tivie held her response which would merely echo earlier discussions between her father and mother. His argument of freeing the slaves and paying them a wage; but collecting rents and selling them supplies, had done nothing to mollify his wife.

"It will come to that, eventually," he insisted. He held up the examples of European practices, even Empires, where slavery had been replaced by freemen – beholden to their masters for their livelihoods.

"What shall we do if the Yankees do forage ashore?"

"There's no need for them to land, providing they get what they want. Besides, we; you, me our neighbors and children, can strike out to St. Augustine and seek sanctuary in the fort. That has stood the test of time and braved the assault of tyrants for centuries," Rebecca emphasized.

Her daughter glanced sideways at the determined profile of the mother of the community. Her own recollection of histories surrounding Castillo de San Marcos, the first stone Spanish fort built in the New World years ago from coquina ferried from dead and buried reefs forming Florida's barrier islands, differed from her mother's. The many races and polyglot voices raised within the city boundaries, did not reflect the rural core of the state.

"Mamma, I do not believe we can rely on the fort to survive a Yankee assault for long. It is not somewhere I would take my family. I would rather chance alligators, bears and snakes than risk their lives under bombardment, or to starve in a siege," she could no long contain her fears for the future. The newly renamed Fort Marion was ceded to America by Spain in 1842 when it finally acquired Florida.

Rebecca spun around, poised to fight, but saw the distress in Tivie's face and heard the mewing of Rosa, crying in her sleep. That retort died on her lips.

"Maybe," she lowered her voice, "there is an alternative, westward," she offered. Other family members had settled nearer the center of the state, further south, near Ocala. The rolling hills were open, unlike the forested lands they occupied, and easier for ranchers to raise cattle.

It was also further away from river or railroad access by Union excursions.

Tivie hushed and rocked Rosa. She gave her mother a grateful nod, then glanced at the shuffling figures strung along the trail.

"What about them?"

"They can fend for themselves. Let them be a burden on the Yankees. See how they like it," Rebecca's responded bitterly.

Chapter 3

Juanita's Woes

America's distinctive raked twin masts, adorned with a medley of green-stuff draped around her standing rigging like garlands on a Christmas tree, were sloped at a shallow angle but above water, when *Ottawa* entered Dunns Creek.

"My Lord. Unbelievable". Her awe-struck captain muttered. Any hopes Lt. Stevens had of keeping her discovery and recovery secret from the crew were dispelled by the leadsman's call.

"By the deep, two, and *America* to port, sir."

His starling break with the traditional call, fetched every set of eyes to focus on the ghostly form most had only heard about, unless they hailed from New York or New Jersey and had seen her during trials so many years ago. The leadsman was beaming with a grin which threatened to crack his face in two when he looked toward the bridge and a flushed Sam.

"Repeat. Correctly this time."

The captain's precise response did little to erase the grinning foredeck crew, or any others who craned to get a first glimpse of the icon, as word swept through the gunboat."Keep a sharp lookout ashore." Stevens scolded. "We are not on a picnic party."

The reminder refocused attention, initially, back to the green curtained layers of slash-pines and cabbage palms, wax-myrtle and magnolia trees poking above head-high mangrove clumps reaching into the shoreline shallows, wrestling for light and water with water hickory and coco plum. An occasional plop of a lazy mullet broke the surface of the brackish water where seeds and leaves floated north on an ebbing tide.

They sensed, but did not see, eyes upon them.

Ashore on Murphy Island, Winston was startled to see his father-in-law on the bridge of the gun-boat, but not surprised. *Juanita*'s presence earlier, under the helmsman-ship of the Cuban, suggested Bryant might have a hand in events. Others among his Florida Ranger's scowled when they too recognized the community's leading figure, but heeded their troop captain's biding to observe and await orders.

Men at the bow-mounted 11-inch Dalgren smooth-bore slowly swung the slightly-elevate barrel between both shores of the islands to either side, tensed and alert. Marines were assembled behind gun-crews peering from loaded cannon, and spotters high in the rigging scanned the shore and terrain beyond.

Ottawa's bristling armament assumed an impact beyond her almost 700-ton 60-plus foot long length easing into the narrow creek. She turned, backing and filling, at the conflux of waters which created a basin between east Florida where Dunn's Creek twisted its way into the lake, with Murphy and Rat islands.

At spots there was little water beneath her nine-foot draft, where her single screw churned clouds of mud and silt from nature's accumulated detritus of the ages. It was swept into the St. Johns River to sink into oblivion or re-establish downstream. Sam's preliminary soundings aboard *Juanita*, together with more details gathered by a brief exploration by the ship's boat, quickly established more men, and a shallow-draft ship, would be required to complete any recovery efforts.

"I propose we return to Jacksonville, picked up more ships boats, round up a diver or two, run a sling under her hull, secure lines to trees ashore and to us – after we set our anchors ashore, and set teams onto the windlass," Stevens looked up from the sketches, charts and tables to the officers who had aired their own opinions.

Sam's proposal to send swimmers into the chill waters to dive and feel her hull for auger holes, plug them then pump her at the Spring low-tide, March 20, was pooh-poohed.

"That'll drown half the crew, tear up their hands on barnacles and pump water back into her – she'll still be underwater," Lt. Vincent protested. "Haul her up, I say."

Other suggestions from inflated cattle-skins to layered rafts of pine trunks died from lack of basic materials, and time.

A jet of steam and the shriek of *Ottawa*'s black-funnel whistle sent flocks of birds whirling into the gray sky a few moments after her captain made his decision. Once they allowed the tide to float her into the mainstream of the St. Johns, he turned over the bridge to Valentine and took the time to pen a report for to Captain DuPont, commander the South Atlantic Blockading Squadron, describing his actions.

~~~

The two Union officers shared an admiration for the prize-winning yacht which was more than just a boat. She represented an ideal of American supremacy afloat.

"*I propose to assemble an armed workforce to include the steamer* Darlington, *the gunboat* Ellen *and the cutter from your* Warbash," *Stevens wrote.* "*While our reception up-river was most amicable from the townsfolk of Palatka; of whom I believe many share our values, there is strong rebel empathy below the pleasing surface which can, with patience, be won over. The former governor is a resident here. He has a large plantation tended by slaves but is not a radical seeking secession as is his successor.*"

The steamer *Darlington* was a former Confederate

side-wheeler which had been captured by Union forces in Cumberland Sound, in the process of transporting army wagons, ammunition and camping supplies for soldiers assembling inland. The Charleston-based ship was maneuverable and of shoal draft suitable for the river communities she was built for. *Ellen* was a sister ship of *Ottawa's* Udilla Class, with duplicate armament and manpower and the cutter from *Warbash*, Dupont's flagship, had accompanied the naval force of small-boats assigned to launch amphibious attacks.

'If our efforts are successful, we shall have the fastest ship, sail or steam afloat, and an icon to parade and rally around," Stevens enthused in the normally formal military correspondence. *"Perhaps we could race her, after the war?"*

For a moment he considered striking his last comment but a hail from above caused him to hurriedly scribble an adieu and sign it before he sealed the letter, thrusting it into the hands of his steward en route, topside.

"What is it?"

Lt. Vincent pointed forward toward the east shore. Two rowers were rapidly approaching land, their oars setting up a spray while their pale faces, even without binoculars, conveyed fear.

While Stevens had been below, *Ottawa* had wound her way north to pass the subdued citizens of Palatka. *Juanita* slipped her tow and with a wave from her skipper Carlos steered for the docks to pick up mail and goods to transport northbound.

Florida's winter sun had decided to make a showing for the day. The metal rail of *Ottawa*'s bridge was warm to the touch, compared to the pre-dawn chill. The white shirts of the rowers seemed to be stuck to their bodies. Through magnification of the glasses pressed to his eyes, Stevens could discern an older and young man, darting glances at the fast approaching shore.

"Should we fire?" Vincent asked.

"We do not want to be the first to shed blood. They present no danger to us. Curious."

"By God. Do not fire, unless you want an international incident," the alarmed voice of trader Bryant called out nearby. He had also peered through a pocket telescope at the fleeing men.

Stevens spun to face him, angered at the civilian intrusion.

"That's Colonel Hemming, an Englishman who settled in Jacksonville decades ago. He's a member of the city council, a prominent auctioneer known throughout the state and the purser aboard the steamboat *Welaka*." The words gushed from Bryant in an anxious torrent. "You could start a war, within a war."

Stevens paused.

"That's his boy, Charles, with him." Bryant snatched a quick glance through his telescope.

All eyes followed the small boat occupants struggle. Faces from the crew turned toward the bridge, urging an order.

"Stand down. Prepare to recover their boat. Keep them in sight as long as you can." Stevens called out. "You'd better be right."

Bryant nodded approvingly.

Ottawa lost way, carried by her own momentum and ebbing tide until she merely drifted on the wide expanse of water north of Palatka. The small boat ran into the shore, both persons tumbled over the bow to splash through the saw-grass onto the bank. They were quickly absorbed into chest-high reeds and brambles, heading north more than east.

Stevens glanced at the hand-drawn map created by the trader Bryant and his Cuban skipper indicating landmarks and landowners along the shore of the St. Johns. It was the first time the name Dr. R. G. Mays, his plantation and saw-mill were brought to his attention.

The gunboat's crew towed the small boat and hauled her aboard, before *Ottawa* resumed course to Jacksonville. Workers along the shore turned their black faces toward her but did not pause in their tasks or wave, as others would have.

"Sir." Lt. Vincent held a jacket recovered from the boat, and flourished an envelope and letter extracted from an inner pocket. A smile wreathed his face like a puppy-dog anticipating a pat on the head.

After a quick glance, Stevens smiled and nodded toward Bryant.

"Seems you were right. Thank you. Lieutenant, you may add a tot to the rations of your men, in addition to any prize-money they may expect from the boat. Join me for dinner, tonight." Stevens dismissed Vincent. "This confirms your British Colonel was hired to sink both the *America* and the steamer. They must have decided to return to Jacksonville."

He smiled.

"If his crew expects to find sanctuary at Fort Marion in St. Augustine, they may be in for a surprise." His eyes met the questioning face of Bryant. "I do believe it will be in our hands by now."

The Spanish-built Castillo de San Marcos had in fact been occupied by Union troops without bloodshed, March 11, 1862, a few days earlier.

~~~

There was some whooping and hollering after *Ottawa* pulled out of Dunn's Creek, until Winston reminded them it was but a brief respite.

"They'll be back, sure as cats sup milk. This could be your last chance to sleep in a bed for a while." He assigned a watch and sent most of his men back to their established base at Bison Bluff, and a few to their homes."

"I ain't gonna be sleepin' if I gits me to a bed," leered a newly-wed trooper.

"Yeah, give yo' hand a chance to heal up, eh?" his buddy jeered.

"Now you mind the time." Winston cautioned. "I want you all back here, this time tomorrow." He glanced at the angle of the sun and the shadows it cast. Few had watches. All knew how to estimate the time, and how to tell north from south from the moss on tree trunks, which grew on the shaded side.

"How 'bout you Colonel, sir?"

"Nope. Not this time. Gotta earn my pay, just like you."

Laugh's greeted his comment. Most wore a mix of gray uniform, had their own weapons and seldom were paid by its cash-strapped Confederate leaders. On their home territory, it worked for them. But they were all aware of scavenging parties sent out to requisition goods from hard-pressed civilians.

"If we do steal from some farmer it's called requisitioning," one Seminole War veteran noted to a new recruit, tin-mug held out for a splash of substitute coffee. "If the Yankee's do it – it's pillaging."

~~~

Ottawa's passage north sent ripples beyond the banks of the St. Johns which rocked *Juanita* at the dock.

Along with the parcels, packages and letters contained in a canvas sack from the citizenry of Palatka and nearby neighbors, she had acquired a couple of notable passengers. Doctor R G Mayes and his foreman Matt McClullough .

They unexpectedly showed up requesting passage to the mill and plantation on the east bank, while their horses were being re-shod by a French master farrier whose skills exceeded the journeyman blacksmith. The ferryman, whose barge connected both shores, had fled with the approach of the gunboat. Some said he was a navy deserter in the past that feared recognition. His barge remained, abandoned, on the far bank with no one to operate it.

"There are no nags available," Dr. Mays nodded across the river. "Drop us off at the mill when you pick up our mail." He jangled coins in his trouser pockets, suggestively. There was no reason Mister Bryant, who stayed aboard the gunship, should know of a little odd-job his boat captain took on.

He would willingly take the dapper doctor aboard, but the scraggly red-beard and brutish-face of the foreman filled him with fear.

Carlos would have done better to bide his instincts. But the bait of a solid gold dollar instead of Confederate script, proved a greater lure for the old buccaneer.

Chapter 4

Recovery

A small fleet crammed into Dunns Creek mid-March, 1862.

Union gunships *Ottawa* and *Ellen* were stationed for protection and assistance while the more maneuverable shoal draft side-wheel steamship *Darlington*, fetched and carried, assisted by small ships boats.

America's masts still cantered to port although successive tides had shifted her hull in the sand and muck creek-bed. Heavy hawsers were counter-weighted , passed under her hull by small-boat crews, bitter ends were returned to the side-wheeler closer to Rat Island and back aboard the gun-boats.

"Just as well they kept her bottom clean for speed, else we'd be sawing those lines asunder," *Darlington*'s skipper commented, carefully following Sam's hand-drawn chart of the hastily prepared creek bottom. One wheel slowly drove forward, the other after, to turn the ship's bow away from land while holding station. Tannin-colored water poured easily in the deeper water; and a slurry of water, weeds and sand slopped off the blades closer to Rat Island.

The process of harnessing the yacht's hull to hold her in a cats-cradle of hemp lines thick as a man's arm, took most of two days.

Every move was observed by Winston and his men.

The temptation to fire was almost palpable. His hot-blooded brother was threatened with physical restraint if he so much as cocked his gun.

"You don't do anything without my say-so. You don't eat. You don't sleep. You don't take a shit. Understand?"

"Yeah, but..."

"No buts. You blood one of them." Winston glared. "I'll take the skin off your back."

Swep had little doubt his normally easy-going older brother would do so. The Colonel had only once caned one of the slaves publicly, for stealing Burrel's Bible. The boy had committed two sins. Stealing and trying to learn how to read. Seeking knowledge, in the eyes of the white community, was worse. Some urged him to blind the boy to teach him a lesson and prevent him trying again.

"Which one of you is going to pay my loss?" Winston asked. "A blind field hand is no good to me. I'd lose two pairs of hands; the boy and his guide. Anybody want to trade me $1,000, hard-cash, to following your advice?"

There were no takers.

An example had to be made. Burrel suggested the punishment most likely to be remembered by all who witnessed it.

Swep was in the front of the semi-circle standing around the saw-horse in front of Tivie's favorite magnolia tree whose white blossoms scented the air, and petals layered the ground. Black and white, separate but together to bear witness, watched the stripling with muscles rippling under his bare back , being led with hands bound before him, toward the place of punishment.

Winston, attired in his military uniform, held a four-foot length of split bamboo cane in one hand, gently tapping the frayed ends into the cavalry-glove on his other. The sound drew all eyes to it while the lead rope was secured low about the tree-trunk, forcing the youth to bend over the saw-bench, balanced on his stomach.

Burell forced a strip of plaited rawhide into the boy's mouth.

"Bite on that, son," he whispered. The wide, terrified eyes implored forgiveness, then naked horror when his britches were removed to the shouts and applause of those assembled who jeered and laughed at the exposure which shriveled his manhood.

The crowd counted down until the last bloody stroke which marked the 18th to match his age, matched the guttural call of a mob. Schoolboy canings, even wood-shed thrashings, paled compared to the pain and humiliation rendered that day. That boy would not be sitting down any time soon to sup, and definitely not to read. Parents who attended, merely threatened to turn errant children over to the Colonel for punishment for peace to reign – for a while – in their households.

Troopers sniggered at Winston's threat and Swep's discomfort. Order was restored in the ranks of Murphy's Island watchers.

There was much coming and going of small boats and shore parties to and from the ships gathered about *America*'s hulk. Lines ran from her to shore and were secured around trunks five feet thick with deep roots spreading wide into Rat Island's soil. The other ends were bound around windlasses aboard *Ottawa* and the other 90-day gunboat, *Ellen*.

Sailors and soldiers in blue and gray bet amongst themselves whether the recovery would be successful or not. The doom-sayer opinions prevailed.

The first attempt to raise *America* was a disaster. Anchor lines on long scopes fore and aft from the gunboats held. The naval store lines held.

They expected the trees to bow, but stand firm. But the deadweight of *America* including ballast plus the tons of water within her hull, proved too much. The trees cried in protest, bending to the tug of the lines. Water cascaded from the tightening strands until, as if on signal, one trunk after another snapped, sending branches crashing and scything through saplings, bracken and brush

America refused to arise. She rocked in place settling back into the mire which held her firm.

The spontaneous cheers of the troopers were drowned under the sound of crashing trees, shouts from the gunboat crews and toots from *Darlington*'s whistle

There were a lot of red faces on *Ottawa*'s bridge, and some ribald comments between the crews of the gunboats which would lead to broken noses and bloodshed should either crew meet in a tavern ashore. Three days lost and nothing to show.

Sam bided his time.

He had discussed the work which had been done on *America* in Jacksonville, with the stoop-shoulder black carpenter, who had since signed on at with the rating of boy, aboard *Ottawa*. Together with others in the chief carpenter's domain, a plan was hatched, involving wood, canvas and caulking. A goodly mound of hemp from old frayed rigging, had been pulled asunder while the carpenters watched recovery efforts.

Captain Stevens' dreams of a triumphant return to Jacksonville with *America* under tow, evaporated with the snap of the tree-trunks. Instead, he may go down in history as the man who destroyed the world's fastest schooner. He could not leave her as she was. His final task would be to render her useless, with a pounding from shells from his gun-boats.

He pondered the problem with a good dollop of whiskey while crew clambered around overhead and ashore, recovering materials so painstakingly placed. A brief knock on the door followed by the immediate appearance of his steward, broke his doleful mood.

"Haven't I told you..."

"Sorry to disturb you, sir," the unctuous tone held no hint of sorrow from the servant who mother-henned his ward. "Lt. Taylor has an urgent message to convey."

With a firm smile in place and a bow of the head he ushered Sam into the cabin, and swiftly withdrew.

"What..."

"If you'll bear with me one moment, sir, there may be a solution before recovery efforts are abandoned, sir." Sam's experience dealing with anxious and irate ships masters, tense at the prospect of handing their charge over to a baby-faced pilot, inured him to a petulant regular navy officer's wrath.

He flourished a handful of loosely-picked hemp, a small role of canvas and a couple of pliable bamboo hoops and a half-hull model of the Yacht *America*.

Intrigued, Stevens rose from his seat, drink in hand, to watch what was being assembled.

Winston watched the renewed activity aboard the lead ship, *Ottawa*, with a frown on his forehead. When the debacle of the broken tree-trunks occurred he had hoped it marked the end of Yankee interest in the area, and they would give up.

But he recalled the determination of his father-in-law, whose livelihood had followed a roller-coaster route like the legendary ice-slides up north and Tivie's inherent stubborn traits.

They watched the collection of navy stores from shore and re-embankment of sailors and hoisting of long-boats aboard, preparatory for leaving. There had been some excitement and uncontrolled whooping from the gunnery crews, about something, followed by ominous activity which could signal a destructive foray into Welaka and surrounding countryside.

Then the captain of the *Ottawa* re-appeared with the young officer who had accompanied Sanchez aboard *Juanita*. A grizzle-haired darky accompanied the group summoned over. Surprisingly, he became the center of attention for a while, then a gawky black-haired olive-skinned youngster clad only in britches was ushered forward. His conversation was accompanied by a windmill of gesticulating arms and hands which reminded Winston of the Italian cook during the Seminole Wars campaign.

He glanced toward Shep who, with everyone else watching, strained his acute hearing to pick up the gist of conversation.

"The kid said something like dive." Shep shrugged.

Within minutes it became obvious to spectators, friend and foe, another attempt was being launched to salvage *America*.

Chapter 5

Phoenix

While the carpenters and sail-makers set about their tasks, Sam ferried the dark-haired youth, an American-born Greek immigrant from the Florida east-coast community of New Smyrna, to the sunken schooner.

Alexandros, with his baby face, large hooked nose, and ready gleaming smile, and the elderly shriveled negro, Jerry, seemed to bond immediately. Some new recruits aboard the pinnace, despite their free-state background, were less friendly.

Sam, who had crewed with sailors of every breed and persuasion in his day, soon learned why.

The Greek, along with the descendants of hundreds from the Spanish island of Minorca and Italians, were part of a colony imported to raise hemp, indigo and sugar-cane, However, dreams of riches in the new world in exchange for their indentured servitude quickly deteriorated to near slavery conditions. They worked in the fields, side by side, with African natives. Each followed the religion of their birthright and, where possible, maintained the rituals and festivals of their homeland.

"Every year, at Epiphany, we boys dove into the ocean

to recover the holy cross. I always won." Alexandros stated the fact without bragging.

"Well, you'll have a chance to prove yourself, and maybe make history." Sam smiled. Their conversation did not escape flapping ears. The crew's attitude shifted, slightly, in favor of the odd couple being ferried to the *America*.

When the tide lowered to the point men could stand on the schooner's submerged deck with water up to the chest, or waist, depending on position, Sam's crew of swimmers slid over the side into the cool March waters of Dunns Creek. Carefully, following directions from Jerry and Sam, the men ducked below the surface to locate hatch openings. They marked the corners with cord, nailed in place if need be, and floating debris recovered from the creek. The sail-locker forward, hatches to the main saloon and ground-tackle aft, were so defined.

Quickly suitable canvas was shaped to size and coils of cord assigned to crew. Then it was the boy Alex's turn to perform.

Tablets of indigo, recovered from supplies the Confederate steamer *Darlinton* had aboard her cargo together with the diver's ability, might provide the first step to recover *America*.

"The carpenter worked on her hull, replacing a sprung plank and caulking her," Sam had explained to *Ottawa*'s captain. "She's got a tough hide and most of the tow-vessel's crew would have high-tailed out of here once she'd been careened. It is his opinion that Colonel Hemming and his son would not have spent as much time piercing her hull before the water in the bilges was too deep. They likely completed the job below her waterline outside, from the dingy we recovered."

Stevens raised an eyebrow.

"If we can put a dye in the water within her, trap it with temporary covers on her hatches at slack tide, the darkest steam of indigo water will seep from those augured holes," Sam explained.

"Pity we don't have Colonel and his boy aboard to question." Stevens pouted. "So, we find the holes, then what? Our efforts to raise her failed."

"Aye sir. Plugging the holes would be our first task. We tried to lift her filled with water. If we make her hull water-tight then slide a tube of canvas or wooden chute into her hatches then extend it above the creek surface, we could jury-rig our ships' pumps to lighten her load." The words tumbled from Sam while the ship's bell tolled the time and Stevens glanced automatically at the ship's chronometer. There was a bit of commotion with voices raised and feet running overhead.

"How much...?" Stevens glanced upward, questioning.

"My men, the diver and carpenters could do it at the next low tide, sir."

"You'd best be right, Mister Taylor. I'm sure we are not alone and cannot understand why the Rebs have not tried something, so far. But all the while we remain gives them time to gather a force to do us harm." Stevens glanced at the surrounding creek greenery.

As if on cue, a gun-shot rang out.

"Hold your fire, hold your fire." The watch officer's call seemed to echo from the banks of Murphy's Island.

Sam stepped aside for the Captain who hastily grabbed his hat to dart topside, and followed.

Yells from the ship mixed with the thrashing broil of bloodied frothed water close to the bank. A figure with a scrap of grayish cloth tied to the barrel of a rifle held aloft, edged toward the water and a fist-sized object moved away from the turmoil, toward him.

"Sambuca" Sam cried, instantly recognizing *Ottawa*'s pet, as had the entire crew urging the struggling feline paddling.

"What the..."

"Cat missed its footing, fell into the creek and the tide swept him away. The log it tried to get to began swimming toward him. It's an alligator." The words tumbled from the watch officer, somewhere between a report and a laugh.

Sam was already shucking off his uniform, barely listening to the explanation, heading toward the side by then.

"Stop him." Stevens called out.

A crowd pressed in upon the officer, no one person laying a hand on him. Sam's head swung from shore to quarterdeck but any utterances he may have made were drowned out by a cheer from all ships when the stranger with the gun scooped the exhausted feline out of the creek to cradle cat, and gun, in his arms.

"Taylor, take your team and a sack of coffee ashore, retrieve that damn cat from the yokel and return immediately to put our plan in effect." The recovery idea had a new owner. "But first, do don your uniform and try to properly represent the United States Navy."

Within minutes the ship's boat touched shore, traded cat for coffee and obliged the scruffy farmer-boy who said he'd been hunting for gators, by recovering the scaly amphibious reptile from a cluster of weeds.

Sambuca leaped into Sam's arms at the sound of his voice, struggling free of his rescuer. The youth did not appear to have begun shaving, had a ready grin and a drawling manner of speaking. However, the rifle he held was immaculate compared to the dusty and patched clothing he wore. The impression of a cap-rim creased his forehead and flattened his hair, but was nowhere to be seen.

He backed off from the water's edge, once the cat left his arms, and deftly caught the small sack with the familiar smell of coffee.

"Much obliged, I'm sure." He glanced at the coffee and gnarled hide of the eight-foot hide lying on the shoreline.

"Many thanks, my friend." Sam could not wave or shake hands, they firmly gripped the purring cat. "And my captain and ship's company extend its sincere gratitude for saving our mascot. Hip-hip..."

The chorus of hurrah's arose from the boat to float into the Florida sky, along with a flight of startled birds at the unexpected noise.

The boy pushed the bow off with his foot, casually cradling his rifle but Sam noticed, the hammer was cocked. He would have liked to spend more time, but as he knew, time and tide waited for no man – and the sunken schooner held priority.

~~~

Minutes later the aroma of fresh-brewed coffee mingled with the fragrance of wild blueberry blossoms when troopers of the Florida Rangers hailed back into the camp and 'requisitioned' the gift from the Yankees.

Winston, wisely, withheld too much recrimination when the circumstances were related to him from many eager tongues prattling praises of the boy who shot the gator to save the cat. The Colonel had been otherwise engaged, downwind from camp, attending to nature's call. The sharp shot heard while he squatted rudely interrupted his ablutions without, fortunately, dislodging his balance. By the time he regained the base the echoes of hurrah's was fading, the boat was pulling away from the bank and a beaming Swep entered the area flourishing the coffee.

"Reckon they knows we're here now," one trooper sniffing the air, nodded with a grin.

"They know *he*'s here," Winston acknowledged as the first hot cup of coffee he had consumed in months was handed to him. He grimaced at the bitter taste, closed his eyes for a split second and sighed with satisfaction.

"Look at 'em, boss," One of his foreign-hired foremen said out of habit, tilting his tin mug toward the men and boats surrounding the sunken ship. "Like fish in a barrel."

"And about as honorable a way to catch 'em." Winston's sense of honor, which had taken the lives of many a Southern gentleman during a dual at dawn, balked at the prospect. "It would be murder, not war."

Though he was in a minority, he ruled.

"Providing we don't provoke any further interest from them our families are safe."

Winston's glance took in Swep, the young marksman with a soft-spot for domestic animals. He was eager to skin and butcher the carcass before buzzards who had got wind of the death, beat him to it.

Together with concealed help they hauled the trophy away from the shoreline with a lasso line. Now, hidden from sight, Shep and a couple of old hands skinned the hide and were busy dividing the meat into portable sizes. Everyone stood to get a portion.

Eyes shifted from the feast to come to activities in the creek.

~~~

The Greek wound inch-long chain-links about his stripling frame, clad only in none-too-clean undergarments. Not an ounce of fat marred his body, chest heaving in a series of heavy breaths while he filled his lungs with air. The additional weight of bound light chain would lessen his buoyancy, he explained.

Together with a few last minute gabbling and hand gestures from Jerry, he lowered himself into the submerged hatch with a small bundle of canvas-wrapped cakes of dye, jack-knifed and disappeared into the opaque waters. The flash of white feet-soles centered within the splash he made, was the last they saw of him.

For a long time.

It seemed, Captain Stevens told Sam later, every man aboard the small fleet, held their breath in concert, willing his safe return.

One minute passed. A long silent pause. Two minutes. There was muttering amongst both sets of onlookers, friend and foe.

Anxiously Sam watched each movement of the minute chronometer's hand jerking around the Roman numbered face with each tick of the hidden movement.

Lt. Vincent's cheroot, which he claimed was a good ten-minute smoke, was down to the stub before the black waterlogged curls of the diver broke the surface again. The tide was low enough for the hazy edge of the hatch to be visible. While all eyes and hands focused on retrieving the gasping Alexandros, a call from one of the sailors assigned to watching *America*'s sunken hull, called out."

"Dye surfacing, sir."

While the diver was bundled into a blanket and tumbled into the pinnace where he was vigorously rubbed dry, a temporary canvas patch was placed over the last exposed deck-opening to contain the colored waters.

A bluish mix of tannin and dye clouded the still ebbing surface. But the waters were slowing. Soon it was placid and the source of the leakage could be estimated. Lines with weights were suspended from the gunwales directly above the darkest concentration. A Jacobs ladder, also weighted, was suspended over the side and the first of a team of swimmers, armed with caulking irons, mallet and chisels, descended to trace the source, and plug it.

Dunns Creek became a liquid shipyard for the next hour and more while a plethora of all ranks and ratings who could swim descended into the murky waters, mallet attached to wrist with a looped cord from handle to wrist, and a net-bag of hemp fibers. The sounds of thumping, muffled by the water, echoed between the islands. Along with shouted orders and the sound of saws, hammers and nails while carpenters constructed tubes to fit into deck openings.

The bluish water dissipated with the blockage of the scuttling holes drilled by Confederates. The incoming tide began to ripple past *America*'s masts and around the legs and torsos of furiously-working carpenters and their mates stripping the temporary hatch-patches off, installing the long tubes and jury-rigged her pumps scavenged from the fleet.

Time was running out for Lt. Stevens' salvaging expedition.

"This is it," he told Sam while he watched and coordinated the recovery team. "She comes up, or she goes down – forever."

Ottawa's gun crews, like destructive children given a box to play with, were anxious to demolish and destroy *America*. It was what they were trained to do.

Sam swayed from the motion of bodies moving about the crowded boat and a light-headed dizziness for uncountable hours of lack of sleep since their arrival. Everyone felt the pressure of racing against the clock, but his anxiety was magnified by the personal attachment he felt for *America*. A world without her was unthinkable.

"All secure, sir," the boatswain relayed the carpenter's comments.

The man and his crew hauling their tool-bags quickly clambered aboard the boat to get shuttled back aboard the gunboats.

Sam joined his shore-crew who would be adding their brawn to the team of men who would take turns manning the pumps.

Soon the sight of two sloping masts, standing rigging and groups of men clustered about the hatches, apparently standing on water, became the focus of all eyes within Dunns Creek, animal and human.

"Commence pumping." Sam called in a firm voice.

Cranking and wheezing contraptions of wood and canvas began moving under muscle power. Bellows squeaked and farty sounds of air being displaced by water heralded the first tentative pints of water filling the void before a narrow dribble, then trickle which turned into a solid gush of purple and blue-tinted water arose from *America*'s guts.

A muffled cheer accompanied the display.

Increasingly, the volume of the tide pressed against the pumpers who implored their mates to brace them against the tug when their feet slid beneath them on the slimy decks.

Sweat dripped to join the swirling, gushing streams of water rising fountain-like to splash into the creek.

Someone aboard *Ottawa* began a sea-chanty used to

raise anchor, which was taken up by many who where not gasping for air, pumping.

The choral chorus was hummed along by Winston's troopers, spectators to the entertainment.

"She MOVES!"

Sam's shrill shout rent the vibrating air – stilling the shanty

America had shifted below his feet.

She was rising.

Part VII

Spoils

Chapter 1

Spoils

In the few hours before dawn, with the grass crisp from ground frost, when brothers, sisters and neighbors bundled together under blankets for warmth in the Rose Cottage camp-site, Winston's horse clopped home for a few hours.

There were no secrets in such confined quarters. Most believed his horse was not the only one who got his oats at the end of their long ride through the woods.

In a hastily created meal of sliced, fire-seared alligator steaks, and real coffee brewed from his portion of the Yankee gift, he brought his refugee family up to date.

"But, they're getting away with it."Rebecca protested. "And you're doing nothing." Her protests did not prevent her consuming her plate of meat or sipping scalding coffee from a common enameled mug.

"Mother Bryant," the timbre of Winston's strained voice was warning enough, for most, he was reaching his limit.

Tivie patted his hand and glared at her mother.

"How many men are there, dearest?" she interjected before any tart response could fan the flames.

Visibly upset, Winston deliberately set his coffee onto the crude surface of the make-do plank table, set up on trestles. His hand was steady.

"There are two gun-boats with their normal complement of one-hundred or more navy and marines, plus additional armed rowers for the extra boats. Then there's the steamer, loaded with contraband seeking sanctuary from their pursuing masters, being taught how to fight. Altogether, twice as many men, women children and hogs as occupy Welaka." He ticked off each amount on the fingers of his hand.

A murmuring and a few gasps from other families occupying the benches of the communal table broke the silence of his litany.

"So to shoot any of them would just be stirring up a hornets' nest." Tivie's comment left no doubt of Yankee reaction. "We would be lucky to escape with our lives and all this–" She waved generally to encompass their sanctuary, crops and livestock, "would be lost."

Rebecca, still glowering, controlled her fiery response. She sensed the mood was akin to her son-in-law and his resolve was reflected by the firm line of his jutting jaw, in the firelight.

Once the issue deflated to where stilted, then lively conversation could continue, he described events at Dunns Creek.

"Young Swep almost brought the war to us because of his passion for animals over people. Him and your Henry," Winston glanced across at his brother-in-law and his old dog Taylor who was finally able to hobble about, recovering from the tree-branch injury.

There was a faint laugh at that.

Winston sensed the audience turning his way. "What does he do, but shoot an alligator to prevent it gobbling up a Yankee cat." He flourished his fork, loaded with meat.

A burst of laughter and cries of alarm greeted his statement.

For the next few minutes, while Tivie gently rubbed his uniformed upper-leg, and more, under the table, he regaled relatives, friends and neighbors with a story which lifted them out of the fear and drudgery of the life they were leading. At the conclusion, when he described the gift of coffee they were drinking, Tivie raised her voice.

"Let's give thanks to the Lord, our Colonel and that devilish boy, for what we have received. And allow my Winston a few minutes to recoup and prepare for his journey back to the front lines. Amen."

A chorus of responses and lifted tins mugs, followed by their departure for the new day's tasks, followed her comments. Rebecca glowered, but remained silent when she departed with a curt nod of her head. She was gracious enough to find a supervisory task far away from the shelter she shared with Tivie which soon briefly became a conjugal nest for the separated couple.

~~~

Shifts of seamen and marines were shuttled back and forth throughout the waning hours of daylight into the twilight, which brought mosquitoes despite the chill air to dawn and buzzing no-seeums who bit before they were seen.

Despite their exposure to raw Florida, as opposed to the glowing reports which encouraged frozen northerners to try the balmy health-giving salty mineral waters and smelly sulfur springs, they avoided the perils of yellow fever. *America* gradually emerged, inch by muscle-stretching inch, from her liquid grave.

Her anchor lines were eased to match her progress. Men plunged into her slimy interior brandishing pine flares carefully when her portholes emerged above water-level to allow air to begin to circulated though her musky hull. Furnishings with cloth were hauled and placed on deck. Blankets and hammocks were hoisted aloft so, from a distance, she look like a ship dressed over-all to celebrate a festive event, or great victory as Lt. Stevens called it.

"We shall make a fine sight for the Confederates to weep over and Unionists to celebrate when we sweep along the river into Jacksonville," he crowed. His eyes swept from the glorious sight of *America*'s familiar silhouette with her classic lines still obvious, despite her unconventional bunting, from the greenery emerging from wraiths of mist hovering above the creek and hugging the shoreline and beyond.

Danger was ever present while they remained within the bosom of the enemy.

The Greek boy was pressed into service once again when *America*'s hull seemed to become sluggish arising. Armed with an assortment of wooden plugs in a net bag, he was sent below water again to hammer them home to give her a more substantial water-tight shell.

The early March morning sun finally reached into Dunn Creek. Cooking smoke from galleys sent tantalizing aromas wafting across the space from ship to shore and beyond setting human and animal nostrils sniffing. The sound of knives and forks scraping against tin or wood platters mingled with conversation and the sound of *America* being pumped back to life.

Her bow wanted to swing to match the tide but anchors fore and aft prevented her from doing so. That movement signaled she was alive, *on* her element.

Sam felt the sway of her deck underfoot and a prideful surge of pleasure at having taken part in saving her.

It was appropriate, once she reached her waterline and was thoroughly examined, to maneuver her on a tow-line run from *Darlington*'s stern, to set off on their triumphant cruise to her new life as a Union ship, to splice the mainbrace. That followed a brief ceremony when Lt. Stevens formally re-named her from her temporary title of *Camilla* to her birthright name *America*, raise the Union flag on her and poured a generous libation into the waters she was about to set forth upon.

The cheers of all who lined the rails rose high above the forests surrounding the ceremony, and broadcast far across surrounding land.

Winston, back from his brief encounter with what passed for civilization, raised his tin mug of coffee in a heartfelt farewell salute.

"We live to fight another day, boys."

~~~

With *Ottawa* leading and *Ellen* bringing up the rear, the image of *America* under the Union-flag towed by a captured Confederate steamer, sent a powerful message to riverbanks east and west and all the communities en route.

That included the plantation of Dr. Mays and his cohorts who fumed at the passing procession. It was not a sight Carlos Sanchez could have seen through his swollen eyelids. Even if he had been free of the chains which held him suspended from the overhead beams of the saw-mill. His recent past, since his abduction, was but a blur of shouted insults interspersed with fist and stick thrashings, the stench of his own body-waste trapped in his bloodied clothes and the buzzing of flies feeding upon open wounds.

His instinct about the plantation foreman was correct.

Once they reached the eastern shore Dr. May offered a tempting gold coin to take *Juanita* the extra mile by water to the bay north of Forest Point where the lawns of the mansion house on the hill ran down to the river's edge and it's colonnaded verandah encompassed spectacular sunsets reflected on the waters.

Carlos was paid and encouraged to step ashore to take a letter from the doctor to his business associates in Jacksonville. He hitched *Juanita* to the extended jetty which ran into deep water and banked the boiler. His dog growled but settled into her sack-bed by the boiler when ordered to do so. Carlos headed toward the mansion, following the foreman in the direction of the kitchen and promise of a meal.

But, they never made it that far.

Once out of sight of the river, Carlos hesitated.

The click of a revolver being cocked and a hail to two stalwart cronies of the foreman, followed by their strong-arm tactics which held him powerless to resist, was the first Carlos knew of his peril. There were plenty who witnessed his plight but none stepped forward. The revolver being flourished between Carlos and anyone standing in their path to the stables, added to their hesitancy.

"Why you do this?"

"Shut yer mouth. We're the ones asking questions."

"What do you want?"

That question triggered the first blow from the empty fist of the foreman. "Shut it, *dago*."

Carlos bristled at the insult but was more concerned about his immediate future.

In the hours following, with the doctor directing the questioning and an occasional slash of his horse-whip, Carlos readily spilled everything he knew of the Bryant patriarch, the family, the whereabouts of the sunken schooner and Union plans to recover it.

The doctor fumed against the Cuban, his foreman and his friends who had aided in thwarting any slave ambitions to escape his plantation, and others within rowing distance, by sabotaging their own boats.

"The blue-coats will do it anyway to prevent us fishing and feeding ourselves," he had argued. "We've got plenty of timber to make-up small rafts to get out of the water; but not big enough to transport whole families."

There was resistance. When some suggested hauling and hiding the boats, the doctor cautioned it would merely signal they were being concealed and encourage troops to land and scour their property. "They might stumble across something more precious than money – the sanctity of your womenfolk and purity of your daughters."

It was enough.

Boats were stripped, holed with axes or burned in plain view so there could be no doubt to any snooping gunboats cruising the St. Johns, there would be no voluntary slaves supplementing their navy from that part of the river.

"Damn. We could have manned those boats and set an ambush at Dunns Creek." The doctor slashed into the battered and bleeding boat captain's suspended figure.

It was with deep chagrin he watched the convoy of Union ships, including the prized *America*, sweep past his home a few days later. Carlos, barely alive, had only been released from bondage long enough to demonstrate *Juanita*'s workings, before being returned to the stable. He was barely able to see through swollen eyelids, but his familiarity aboard the boat allowed him to reach for valves, gear-levers and whistle-pull even in the darkest night.

It spared him the sight of his dog, secured and helpless, when her throat was cut. The final yelp and smell of spilled blood when the carcass was flung over the side filled his nostrils.

When Mays' men hauled him back to captivity, tears coursed a path through the grime on his cheeks. Then he heard his livelihood clank her familiar tune, fade into the distance when she was fired up and run into the concealing marshland east of the mansion.

The tears flowed freely to sting his cut lips, murmuring curses and vengeance against Mays and his men.

~~~

A barrage of distant gunfire roused James Bryant from his bunk aboard DuPont's flagship at Mayport, where the remnants of the blockade squadron lay safely anchored in the deep-water bay between Jacksonville and the Atlantic Ocean.

A series of sporadic single shots and ships bells, whistles and cheers grew closer with the approach of the gunboat *Ottawa* leading his prize vessel which, through semaphore sites between shore and ship, signaled *America*'s arrival.

Bryant was joyful and agitated when he joined the blockade squadron's leader on the bridge forming the impromptu welcoming committee. Wherever there was a ship, or a Unionist ashore, hoots and hollers and small arms firing into the sky greeted *America* as word rippled along the gossip grapevine. The trader had to wait his turn before the DuPont relinquished the hero of the day after his formal pose before

America and her bizarrely draped masts. Lt. Stevens plus Sam and others grouped before the bedraggled silhouette of the recovered yacht, now flying the Union flag.

It was not until the second wave of congratulations and introductions began that Bryant managed to catch the eye of Sam and pushed through well-wishers to clasp his hand.

"Well done. What a magnificent accomplishment. I'm so happy to see you all alive and well." Bryant wrung the young officer's hand.

"It was touch and go. Especially when I met your kinfolk, face to face." Sam's lopsided smile indicated more than a social encounter.

"How is the boy?" Bryant immediately responded then realized, they should not have encountered each other. "Is he...?"

"He's fine, sir, and so is Sambuca, my cat." Sam's smile spread.

"Thank the Lord." Bryant's eyes lifted skyward before his single-minded purpose returned. "I fear for the safety of *Juanita* and her captain, Carlos Sanchez."

It was Sam's turn for eyebrows to raise.

"A freedman, who also plies the St. Johns in a cat-boat, delivered some disturbing news to my temporary office at the old Confederate newspaper office, abandoned but intact when y'all arrived." The southernism had crept unnoticed by him, into his Yankee speech.

"He said he had seen *Juanita* taken into the marshes behind Dr. May's plantation – but Carlos was not at the helm. I fear that Reb firebrand may have strayed from free-speech into vigilante territory."

His agitated talk which rose with passion caught the attention of those about him including *Ottawa*'s commanding officer who had just completed reporting how he had subdued resistance in the Palatka area.

The pinprick, which deflated his pride of the moment, had Lt. Stevens, bristling.

"How can you suggest such a thing? I have just returned from a most successful foray into enemy territory and returned unscathed, as you can see." He waved toward the open scuttle wafting celebratory cigar-smoke from the wardroom to *America*'s presence.

"I have no doubt you were well received and fussed over in a friendly manner,"Bryant tried to placate *Ottawa*'s captain. "We Yankee merchants were smothered in southern hospitality and seemingly the closest of friendships, until this plague of slavery and secession caught hold. Now we seek sanctuary and look back upon the ruins of our lives and no way to tell friend from foe."

Bryant's impassioned comments silenced the celebratory conversation.

"You are saying your man, and your boat, are being held hostage?" Captain DuPont, anticipating promotion following his wave of successes which had established Union bases for a blockading fleet along the southern Atlantic coastline, and recovered the iconic yacht on his watch, glanced at Stevens.

"We leave for Palatka immediately, sir, at your pleasure," the gun-boat captain, anticipating the command, responded with alacrity.

"Make it so."

Flag Officer DuPont's ritual response gave his chagrined gun-boat captain all the leeway he could hope for.

Chapter 2

Retribution

Panic pervaded the plantation when the solid shape of USS *Ottawa* emerged from the morning mist dispersing with the arrival of a new day in Palatka.

There was something different to the rhythm of life which roused Mays from his slumbers well before the insistent knocking on the bedroom door and his gray-faced butler announced: "There's a battleship with its guns pointed at us, on the front lawn, suh."

"Don't be ridiculous Noah." May flung back the imported eiderdown and fluffy linen sheets to emerge from bed in an ankle-length flannel nightgown over his head to foot underwear. He thrust wool-stockinged feet into rabbit-skin slippers and shuffled across the carpeted hardwood floor to the shuttered west window.

A comment died stillborn when he peered through the slats overlooking the lawn, his wife's magnolia tree with bench, table and chairs loosely assembled around it, to the lawn's edge, the river and indeed, a ship ready for battle with a display of cannon pointed directly at him.

"Good God!"

His expletives which followed aroused his wife's silk night-capped head from the comfort of the covers.

"What is it dear?"

"Those damn Yankees are back. With a ship. And its guns are aimed at us,"

His words were interspersed with grunts and gasps while he hastily donned his clothes, grabbed his night-stand pistol and clumped in knee-high riding boots, to head outside to meet his foreman.

"What's going on here?"

"Don't rightly know, Doctor Mays, sir. They just appeared."

There was concern on the face and in the voice of foreman McClullough who clutched a musket in both hands. His customary whip was coiled over his right shoulder, ready if needed. Other team-leaders faced slaves who emerged on the path leading from their quarters, a collection of huts out of sight of the mansion. Seemed to Mays, who glowered in their direction, most of the eighty-eight men, women and children he owned, had gathered.

"Get them back to the quarters. No one leaves for the fields, understand?" He turned his attention back to the ship which he had viewed from his bedroom.

The crack of whips and thump of cudgels followed by wails of protest, faded while his orders were followed. Together with his core and his absent partner's people, he strode down to the dock where the family row-boat and day-trip sloop were tied up.

For a moment he regretted his weak-kneed partners had abandoned him for their kin in Charleston until the quick war was over. They were more suited to soothing words and social games he sensed would be required, soon.

"They're loading a small boat, with a white flag," the foreman observed aloud.

"I'm not blind, man," Mays snapped. He reached into his coat-tail pocket and extracted a white, but snuff-stained, large linen handkerchief and languidly waved it overhead a few times.

~~~

Lt. Stevens crumpled the letter he had written en route to the plantation to begin again, a less conciliatory correspondence. He no longer questioned whether the steam-launch captain was being held by the doctor.

Ottawa's silent approach to the plantation had been achieved by a combination of sail and an in-flowing tide which swept the gunship south up the St. Johns wide expanse with the aid of the prevailing spring north-east wind. They were mere yards away from their designated anchorage, about to swing into the tide and wind, when a makeshift log platform bearing a lone fisherman, was spotted.

He held a casting net in both hands. A small barrel with a board across it to retain splashing finger-mullet for bait perched between the bound logs. His face lit up, his cast turned into a wave of joy. He trust a sturdy bamboo pole into the mud below and held his craft in place, watching.

Stealthily boats loaded with anchors fore and aft were loaded on greased pulleys onto the river, the crews pulled, paying out chain scope as quietly as possible to set the anchors without noise or fuss. The fisherman, barefoot but bundled against the chill sunrise hour, braced his raft against the bending but sturdy pole, silently watching.

Jerry, the old carpenter who seemed to dog Sam's footsteps whenever he was not involved in a task, watched closely. When the evolution was completed and *Ottawa* lay wreathed in mist a few hundred feet from the plantation heart, the boats returned. One towed the insistent fisherman whose rising voice threatened their presence.

"What is that man up to?" Vincent hissed.

"He wants aboard."

"I can see that, Mister Taylor. But why is he so noisy?"

"He gots news from the house 'bout the Cubano." The carpenter's voice reached out from behind Sam's uniform.

Vincent's eyes moved from Sam's face to the old man.

"How'd you know that? Who gave you permission to speak?"

"He from the Gullah. Alla fella from de islands." The carpenter's hands waved northward.

"The barrier islands off Georgia and the Carolinas," Sam explained.

"What's all this?"

Stevens thrust his way into the fiercely whispering group gathered at the boarding port. Quite an audience of loafers had built around the core of conversation.

The scrap wool multicoloured tamashanty-styled cap of the lone fisherman poked level with the deck, followed by his broad smile and bundled long body. His jabbering began immediately.

"What the...?"

"He's talking a mix of English and African, sir," Sam said. "I can pick out a few words. He's talking about the 'bad mans' and 'the *Juanita*' and..."

"All right, all right. Let's take this off the deck. Into the galley," Stevens urged. "Boson, clear the decks – quietly."

A line was run down to secure the raft and its barrel-load of splashing contents, then run aft of the gun deck ports, leaving the ship's boats free for their next task.

In the galley, which seldom saw such distinguished company except during Captain's Rounds, the cook's ears absorbed as much as possible between pouring coffee into hastily scoured enamel mugs. The fisherman's eyes were wide at the opulence displayed. His nose twitched at the spices and aromas wafting about the tiny kitchen. He had never entered such splendor. He always handed his catch to the cook's aide, at the dock.

During the following minutes, using the carpenter and Sam as interpreters, Stevens was able to piece together the situation ashore. And the consequences for the future of the plantation, its owners and slaves.

~~~

While the occupants of the big house still slumbered and the overseers and their families stumbled out of bed, a boatload of leatherneck marines under their lieutenant and Sam's crew of roughnecks were steered ashore by senior midshipmen. The lone fisherman and *Ottawa*'s newest carpenter guided the marines to the white, armed, section.

Sam scoured the marshes for *Juanita*. He was looking for upright poles, topped by wide-mouth ginger-beer bottles, marking passage into the run-off stream giving access to her hidden mooring.

They passed a pool of logs loosely rafted recent arrivals floated to the saw-mill. He noted several two and three-log rafts suitable for poling into the shallows for bait catching, and fishing, similar to the craft they saw earlier. The remnants of holed and burned boats lined the shores.

The false-dawn gave them enough light to see the shoreline and details emerge before the weak March sun made its appearance. Sam shivered, not just from the chill, when the shape of the stables and smithy shop emerged. That's where Carlos was reported to be.

"Marker to port, sir," a hoarse whisper from a

crewman, hand pointing over the port bow, indicated the furthermost pole crowned by a frosted bottle glistening, ahead.

The midshipman adjusted the helm. Rowers feathered their oars. Hands gripped rifles more firmly, their owners alert to any opposition. Their instructions were to creep aboard, overcome any guard, secure the steam-boat and silently tow her away from the plantation and rifle-range. Icicles hung from her frost-covered awning, but heat from her banked boiler kept water-jacket and pipes free from rupture.

Sam who had observed and assisted Carlos on their trip to and from *America*'s scuttled location, noted she appeared in well-founded condition, her fuel-box loaded with extra bundles neatly stacked beside it.

"She's all ready to go, somewhere," he said.

The fresh-faced Midshipman nodded, as did Murphy from the shore squad.

"Let's get outta here, sir," he urgently pressed, glancing apprehensively at the raw territory so alien to his Baltimore streets.

"Just a moment. Turn about, Middy. You men, get a line on her. Haul her anchor up, softly. You, and you, get aboard with me. Haul us out, quick as you can."

As quietly as possible bodies moved aboard and between the two boats. A few bird protest calls were the only notice paid to their activities they were aware of. Other eyes, just above the water's surface, watched every move from the mud-caves created in hammocks on the creek's fringes.

Juanita eagerly responded to the tow-line and swung in behind the ship's boat.

Under Sam's direction the men coiled twenty-foot long lines inboard and secured them to her ribs, where possible.

"Just in case." Sam offered no further explanation to the puzzled looks he got.

Quietly and methodically, he practiced the paces he would need to take to engage *Juanita*'s engine and gears to bring her alive.

~~~

The marines were too late to capture or engage the menfolk of the small white enclave. The lieutenant advised the women to pack what they could, secure their children and retreat eastward toward the main trail ford St. Augustine.

"For how long?" an irate, aproned grand-motherly figure demanded, hands on hips and a long-handled wooden spoon held defiantly.

"Ma'am, I wouldn't come back until all is quiet."

"What do you mean?"

"You'll know, ma'am. You'll know." He managed a tight smile on his stern youthful face.

The body of troops behind him looked anxious but determined. It was enough.

"C'mon boys, girls. We're off for a picnic. Get your blankets, and toys, pots, plates. Hurry, hurry."

The spoon was brandished, squeals and laughter rang out and little legs scampered to obey. Within a few minutes the small cluster gathered outside. With a doleful glance at their Florida homes, the parents led a cotillion of children along a path many had seldom traveled, escorted for part of the way by armed uniformed men who cautioned them not to return.

Gunners aboard *Ottawa* maneuvered her weapons where they were pivotable, taking elevation readings and sightings of all the structures representing potential targets.

The fat howitzer borrowed from *Warbash* was packed

with decimating canister and grapeshot in case there was any attempted assault by massed small boats. The two 20-pounder Parrott rifle-cannon and chubby iron-belted smooth-bore swivel Dahlgren were readied to rain destructive fire upon any cannon, ship or structure which opposed it. Her two 24-pound conventional cannons on carriages, poking out from either side, would lend their weight, if needed.

Everything depended on the rebel doctor's response to Lt. Stevens' letter demanding return of Carlos Sanchez.

Chapter 3

Exodus

Rumbling like thunder alerted the citizens of Palatka and others along the liquid highway of the St. Johns River of something amiss that clear, blue sky morning, mid-March, 1862.

For many it was the first time they ever heard the sound of the Civil War.

The sound carried far. But the deed reached every corner of the far-flung state within days.

Union troops freed slaves and demolished a thriving plantation because one man was hanged.

~~~

Shortly before what would have been breakfast time at the house overlooking the St. Johns, soon after Dr. Mays read Lt. Stevens' demand for the release of the abducted boatman– or else–there was movement ashore.

"They're bringing someone out, with a sack over his head." The adolescent voice of an excited midshipman, perched high in *Ottawa*'s shrouds with a telescope, carried on the water.

All eyes, with and without magnification, peered at the white-columned building facing them. The tall, smartly dressed doctor stepped down from the balustraded porch onto a crushed shell-rock path leading to the water, the jetty and his wife's favorite tree. A group of white men frog-marched the stumbling, shackled, masked man from the stable-side of the building, headed for the tree.

"My God. They're going to hang him."

Lt Vincent glanced ashen-faced toward *Ottawa*'s captain. Sam, amongst those few on the bridge, nodded slowly, focused on the figure. The blood-stained familiar tan-colored shirt-jacket the Cuban always wore, confirmed who the captive was.

"It's him, sir. Carlos Sanchez."

"They may be delivering him..." Stevens' voice tailed off when the parties headed for the tree instead of the jetty. One man broke away to fetch a chair from the garden furniture.

Stevens snatched the hailing trumpet from its hook, automatically wiped the grit and salt from the mouthpiece and bellowed into it.

The tinny sound of his voice could be heard by all aboard and ashore.

"Unhand that man. Bring him to the dock – or suffer the consequences."

The group ashore ignored the order. One stood upon the chair to pass a sturdy rope, with a noose at one end, across a stout branch about eight feet above ground where it branched out.

It was as though Mays dared the Union Navy to take any action.

Carlos was lifted into the chair. One man held it steady, two braced his swaying body, another placed the loop around his neck and secured the bitter-end with two-turns around the tree-trunk.

Dr. May faced the ship and cupped his hands.

Talk, which had reached a higher pitch as everyone on deck commented about the scene ashore, stilled while all strained to catch his words.

"Leave my land, or he dies." He nodded to his foreman to take up the slack.

None could say whether he misunderstood or if a spasm of pain twisted Carlos's broken body. In an instant the chair was overturned. May's arms flailed to his men at arms to support the Cuban's body. But they panicked, scattering, leaving the thrashing body to jerk spasmodically against the tightening noose.

A moment frozen in the minds *Ottawa*'s crew for all time.

Without consciously considering his actions, Sam snatched the rifle from the gazing guard, sighted upon the swaying body, and fired.

Wherever the shot landed – the body stilled, slumped to sway on the rope's end.

In that split second of silence, May's wail of realization carried across the water.

Stevens never hesitated, even to scold Sam.

"Fire!"

His order rent the Florida air in flame and fury. The boom and smash of a broadside accompanied by a scything whistle of firearms wounding, maiming and slaying all within sight, turned the pastoral green lawn and white structure into a hell-on-earth in the blink of an eye.

Miraculously Mays survived the fire but not the humiliation.

By darting behind the tree-trunk to then scamper from its cover toward the shelter of thorny bushes and sharp marsh grasses edging the lawn, he escaped death and capture.

The cease-fire was not sounded until all buildings; house, stables, saw-mill and out-buildings, were reduced to rubble and matchwood.

No bodies were found when the flames died down and *Ottawa*'s men explored ashore. They recovered the hanged Cuban to transport back to Jacksonville, James Bryant, and many of Carlos's surviving relatives.

Juanita, under Sam's hand and the ever-intrusive Sambuca plus his shore-party, set out lines to slaves who opted to be towed on makeshift log rafts in the steam-launch's wake.

Stevens' report to DuPont expressed regrets he had been unable to retrieve the abducted man, alive, but believed the example made of the destruction of one of the most powerful slave-owning planter's in Palatka, would curb any future vigilante or malicious militia action in the area.

He was wrong.

ooOoo

Cast of Characters

America's Race, Great Britain

Cookie – *America*'s cook.

Bambino – Sammy's cat.

Colonel James Hamilton – syndicate member, son of American Secretary of Treasury.

Commodore John Cox Stevens – New York Yacht Club leader of syndicate

George Schuyler – New York Yacht Club member of the syndicate.

George Seers – brother of designer.

George Seers II., - nephew of yacht designer and crew member.

Her Majesty Queen Victoria – monarch of England. Pet name Drina by husband

James Seers – yacht designer, connoisseur of wine, imbiber of commodore' liquor.

Marquise of Angelsey – one-legged hero of Waterloo and avid yachtsman.

Prince Albert – German-born husband and Consort to the queen.

Richard 'Dick' Brown – yacht's Master and Captain of the New York pilot boat *Mary Taylor*

Sammy, Samuel, Sam Taylor – stowaway and ships boy (Later USN officer).

***The St. Johns River. Florida* - and its Civil War players**

Calvin Robinson – Yankee merchant and saw-mill owner in Jacksonville.

Captain (Colonel) Winston Stephens – Plantation owner and husband of Octvia living at 'Rose Cottage, Welaka. Former Seminole War cavalryman, Officer in charge of independent Cavalry Troop based in East Putnam.

Carlos Sanchez – former Cuban buccaneer and skipper of Bryant steam launch *Juanita*.

Colonel Hemming – English migrant resident Jacksonville councilman and auctioneer.

Dr. Ralph Mays – one of three partners of a large plantation worked by second largest slave group in Putnam county. Southern supporter of Secession.

Burrel – Head slave on 'Rose Cottage' plantation, possible half-brother of Winston Stephens, pastor and schoolmaster within plantation family.

Former Florida Governor William Moseley, first statehood leader, resident of Putnam County, planter and biggest slave-owner in region.

Henry Bryant – younger brother of Octavia. Boy soldier with brother-in-law's troop.

James Bryant – Northern publisher, merchant, entrepreneur founder of Welaka community. Federal supporter.

Mrs. Marion – chaperon

Octavia 'Tivie' Bryant-Stephens – daughter of Welaka founder, wife of sourther planter and Confederate Troop Captain.

Rebecca Hall Bryant – merchantile family wife of Welaka founder. Southern supporter.

Swepson Stephens – Captain's younger brother, sharp-eyed marksman, keen-eared hunter.

United States Navy

Alexandros – Greek boy free-dive record holder from New Smyrna colony.

Brian Hawkins – Union spy.

Capt. Samuel DuPont – Commander of the South Atlantic Blockading Squadron.

Jerry – black carpenter, Jacksonville boatyard.

Lt. Samuel (Sam, Sammy) Taylor – *America* stowaway, Sandy Hook pilot, surveyor then *Ottawa* navigator

Lt. Thomas Holdup Stevens Jr. Captain of gunboat *Ottawa.*

Lt. Valentine – Captain of US Coastal Survey schooner *Jersey II.*

Lt. Vincent – First Officer aboard *USS Ottawa.*

Nautical Terms and Slang

'eavo, 'eavo, 'eavo, lash-up and stow - command for crew to get up, bundle hammocks and store them.

Aft or Stern – back end of vessel.

Beam reach – when wind is directly blowing against one side of vessel, or the other.

Blocks & tackles – a contraption using wheels and ropes to raise and lower sails,etc.

Bob-stay – line or chain below bowsprit to hull waterline preventing upward lift.

Bow – front of boat

Bosun (boatswain) – a senior rating on the lower-deck (think senior sergeant).

Bowsprit – a spar extending forward of the hull to provide a mast anchor point and foresail rigging.

Capstan bars - turning the capstan to raise the anchor was done manually using brute force against wooden spokes inserted into the ratcheted windlass device.

Cats paw - a light ruffle on the surface of water by a sudden breeze.

Cleat – a mounted wood or metal device allowing a line to be secured.

Cockpit – the location from which a vessel is steered

Cutter rig – Single masted sailboat supporting all sails on one mast. A sloop.

Deck – floor

Ebbing tide – waters going out

Flood tide - waters coming in

Flying jib - an additional sail located before the standard forward sail.

Flying jib boom - additional boom extending beyond the bowsprit.

Fore – front of vessel.

Gybe – when a wind-filled sail crosses from one side of the hull to the other. An uncontrolled change can be devastating.

Halliard – a line to hoist a signal or national flag.

Hold – space for cargo, stores

Jury-rigged - a makeshift emergency repair.

Keel – lowest part of vessel; the spine upon which the ribs rest.

Keel shoe – metal shield to protect wooden keel from damage by rocks or reefs.

Lay line – a course set to reach a destination taking into account tide and wind.

Leech – end edge of sail nearest helmsman.

Lollygagging – lazy, slacker, ne'er-do-well

Luff - sail flutter caused when wind flow across front and back surface of sail.

Mudlarks – Victoria children who scavenged for scraps along shoreline and mudflat of London's River Thames.

Pilot – seaman with local knowledge of tides, sand bars and reefs and safe passage routes.

Pitch – dip of bow into waves slowing forward motion.

Port – left side, while facing bow.

Quarterdeck – usually a raised deck area at the rear when the vessel is steered from.

Schooner – a sailing vessel with two masts

Sea-legs – ability to move in sync with motion of vessel without ill effect.

Set of the sails – whether sails are taut and filled with wind or sagging

Sheets – rope or cordage used to adjust position of sail position from port to starboard.

Slack water – period when tidal flow ceases to rise or fall.

Slipways – slope between land and water where braced vessels can be worked on at low-tide.

Sod's Law – sailors believe a challenge to Davy Jones can spark disaster by making a positive statement about a vessel's prowess.

Standing rigging – ropes permanently securing masts.

Starboard – right side, while facing bow.

Stays – lines fore and aft securing mast tops.

Tack – change of course and direction to allow a boat to progress against the wind.

Tarry – dawdle

Transom – back of a boat.

Tuned – angle of masts, tautness of lines holding them in place, position of sails, balance and rudder for fastest speed.

Wherry – boat built to carry passengers from ship to shore.

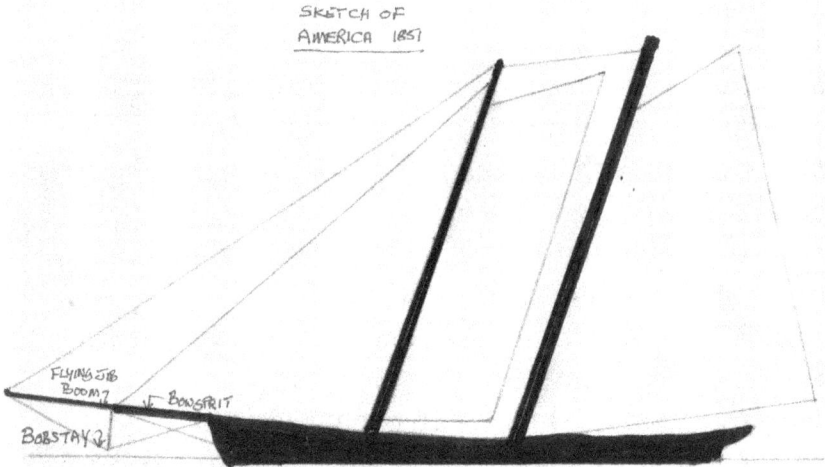

SKETCH OF AMERICA 1851

FLYING JIB BOOM

BOWSPRIT

BOBSTAY

www.ingramcontent.com/pod-product-compliance
Lightning Source LLC
Chambersburg PA
CBHW022005090426
42741CB00007B/896